FINDING A
NEW LIFE

FINDING A
NEW LIFE
to Change
Our World

DANIEL GABRIEL

Finding a New Life to Change Our World
Written by Daniel Gabriel

ISBN-13: 978-0-9978410-6-0
Library of Congress Control Number: 2018949285

Dedication

To my mom, dad, and to the Lord God for
working through many people to provide me
with food, water, and shelter on my journey.

TABLE OF CONTENTS

INTRODUCTION

This is a true autobiographical story of a young man's adventurous cross-country journey into the unknown, going halfway across the United States on a 10-speed bicycle, driven by motivation surpassing thoughts of whether I would live or die trying to make it to the final destination.

A tough start occurred when no one else would dare go on the trip, and the decision was made to do the trip alone. This also meant severing from city life and terminating a job as a building engineer for the Wright Building in downtown Tulsa, Oklahoma, to pursue my desire to explore a new world.

I rode 1500 miles on a 10-speed bicycle through snowstorms with very little provisions, encountering insurmountable odds, which made for impossible scenarios for survival or success. The unexpected happened, and sometimes life gets out of control.

Only you can imagine if you could possibly accomplish the different challenges of this exciting exploration by reading about my numerous experiences along the journey to San Diego, California.

Sometimes in life, we really need to have an active imagination to drive us to be ambitious. With a vision of excitement, we can open the arena to see if our expectations and dreams can come true.

CHAPTER 1

JUMPING OFF THE CLIFF

When I was a teenager, every time I turned on the radio, I heard the popular song, "What the World Needs Now Is Love, Sweet Love." It is so wonderful to say and so delightful to hear, but we have to have love in ourselves to change our world by giving it away freely. Some people have received love from others. Some people are drawn into an inherent discovery of sensing they feel good, showing and demonstrating charitable acts of kindness that develop into a love to show others. Maybe we can find that pursuing love is our main purpose in life.

One day, a driven desire to have a changed life was like jumping off a cliff for me. In my case, once I jumped, it wasn't possible to be retrieved from entering into a world of the unknown. As I came from a well-encased secure family background, I felt my teenage roots were causing me to become a big city fan. This was preventing me from experiencing a different kind of life. From the time I was eleven, I developed a love for the thrill of riding motorcycles, rebuilding engines, camping, and playing sports.

This shaped my character earlier in life, compelling me go into assistant building engineering at age eighteen. All of these things in my life became insignificant to me when I discovered that a whole world is out there that I had not explored. Curiosity gave me a desire to find a new world. How does it sound to throw it all away and jump on a 10-speed, ride from Tulsa, Oklahoma, to San Diego, California, in the snow, just for a change? Is it insanity, too risky, or would I ever live to tell the story?

What would follow is my dive off the cliff, which literally was plunging myself out of the garage, into a snow blizzard, on a 10-speed one extremely cold Monday morning in the last part of November, not knowing if I would ever return to Tulsa again. There were reasons making it impossible to return. For one, I felt compelled to have the bravery to tackle the momentous 1500-mile trip or I could be branded a coward for rest of my life. Second, the world was an open door that I had to pass through at that moment in time, never to reoccur again for me in my lifetime. Third reason, I had made a commitment to go into the Marine Corps the next month to serve my country, and if I didn't make it, I would be AWOL, unauthorized absence, and would not stand as a qualified recruit. Fourthly, this became my life test to physically take the challenge to be validated and recognized.

If ever in life your world was handing you what most people would cherish as a great life to build upon, then you go out like a misguided missile, and you're probably looked at as pretty crazy to give it all up. Snow and ice causing slippery accidents from a passing motorist running into me could end my life on the front bumper of any car trying to pass me, and I might never see them coming. But the journey of no return had begun with the attitude that as long as I could stay on top of two wheels or push my way through the snow, I was going to reach out in front of me for every inch of the 1500 miles.

I fishtailed down the roads as I peddled the weighty bike, loaded down with clothes, food, tools, and a backpack. I had so much in luggage, such as two side bags, a handlebar bag, and a sleeping bag at the back of my seat, that it looked like I was riding a slow-moving motorcycle.

The first day started with a cold sluggish pelting of falling snow, which impeded any advancing momentum. The one-inch-wide tires on my French Jeunet bike were slicing through the thick blankets of white fluff. The only scenic objects were the moving things—cars, people, and sparrows flittering through the snowflakes. Being far from home and far from setting any kind of land-speed records, I had resigned any attempts to find something with any kind of shelter.

Ah ha! I found a carport at the side of a closed filling station that could give me relief from the falling snow. I rolled out the sleeping bag while the snow was falling that night. It felt good just resting from the full day of pumping the pedals. I became intrigued with everything being snow-covered; yet the reflectivity from the white glowing clouds and the surface of the snow displaced the darkness at night. I slept with one eye open, not knowing if the owner of the station would roust me out and force me to spring into action.

The first sign of morning light caused me to react in paranoia that catapulted me out of the carport lightning fast. It was impossible to cover my tracks and the fact that I had lodged there overnight. I grabbed some fruit out of my handlebar pack and continued to head down Route 66 to the West. Reality struck me, as I recalled the saying, "Go West, young man, go West," referring to the meaning that your life could have a better outcome, happier life, or more fortunes to discover at the risk of losing it all.

Pedaling downhill at a good clip caused the cold air to slap my cheeks, which became the caffeine jolt that I needed to get my legs going early in the morning.

Then, after thirty minutes of a brisk pace, I became more awakened to the fact that achieving more forward momentum caused me to reach for all the gusto, wanting more and more progress.

The winter's cloudy, overcast skies seemed to make the day so long. Without seeing the sun for a reference of time, it was very difficult to know if I could reach Oklahoma City by the second night. I barely made it to a roadside park with a men's restroom, which had the best shelter from the cold snow. Even though it was extremely strange to be sleeping on the floor of a restroom, it was also quite embarrassing when strangers had to step over me to use the toilet during the night. Nevertheless, the warmth was enough to overcome the inconvenience. I was awakened in the middle of the night by a rude kick to the biscuits—with some rough-sounding guy saying, "Are you alive?" I woke up and yelled back, "Hey, man! Watch it!"

The morning didn't come soon enough to relieve me of the homeless label that people thought of me, but then I had to dart back out into cold snow again. Getting onto Route 66 now became my lifeline connection to a new life. The sights I saw were new discoveries, recorded in the camera of my mind, remembered for a lifetime and yet became history as fast as I pedaled past them, which may be stored or replayed from a "10-speed point of view." As I was going through El Reno, Oklahoma, on Route 66, I realized the outside of the road for safely trying to ride a bike was really only as wide as the white stripe at the edge

Leaving the Safety of Home. I grew up in a traditional American family home with my mom, dad, and younger sister. *Left:* me, Leamon, and Betty holding Sheila. *Right:* My parents, Leamon and Betty.

of the road. There was a very narrow margin of error. It was extremely difficult to distinguish the white line due to the snow. If I veered a little to the left off the white line, I was afraid that I would become game for the oncoming cars to make me road kill. If I veered a little to the right, I could slip off into the rocks and end up in disaster. I never knew that I would encounter such hazardous conditions.

A long hard day's ride brought me past an old historical steam locomotive with a caboose and a teepee at the Old Town Museum in Elk City. I was about out of steam myself and thought how nice it would be to sleep there tonight. Naw! I better not change history by having a modern biker make it look like a drive-in motel. Instead, I forced myself to the next area in the dark where there was a tiny park with a picnic table and a cookout grill. It had a pole light shining so that I could see to roll out my sleeping bag on top of the table and under the thick fluffy clouds. This was better than any teepee or motel room with this table providing a nice, dry, hardwood bed. I had myself convinced that I had it made for the night and nothing could be better to give me the best sleep in comforting fashion.

At some point during the night, the clouds unzipped and I was awakened as fast as I went to sleep by a shocking white mask. Freezing snow had fallen while I was asleep and made my face look like the abominable snowman. "Oh shoot! Everything is a complete mess!" I thought. I leaped up like a jack-in-the-box, wiped the snow off my face, brushed it off my sleeping bag, pulled my boots on, and packed in the early morning darkness, being miserable. I took off, being disgusted, until I saw a glimmer of light in a diner a quarter of a mile down the road that was open early on this dark morning. What a relief to be able to have the taste of a hot breakfast and the taste of civilization again, after feeling pretty stiff from the cold and wild looking from not shaving. Most people probably thought that I was pretty crazy, riding a bike through the snow for such a long distance. People didn't quite know how to react to me—you just never saw anyone ever try a 1500-mile bike trip in those days.

When my best friend Ricky Gibson and I were both twelve, we got up at 5:00 am on a Sunday morning to go fishing. We strapped our fishing poles to our 20-inch bikes and headed to Lake Yahola. This was our first major trip we had ever been on. This was a whopping five miles going one way north of Tulsa. Our goal was to see who could catch the biggest fish and have the most incredible fish story to tell. We did more poking at each other and sword play than catching fish. You know at certain times in life, you must find out what you're capable of achieving, along with discovering what aspirations you may have that can excite you and catapult you into action. Your energy can be bubbling over and ready to burst out to drive you into making your vision come true. Will it be for pleasure in self-fulfillment or pursuing a productive goal of helping others in their accomplishments of big business?

As the snow started to fade away with the glimpses of a few rays of sunshine coming through the overcast, I saw the first significant milestone starting to pass in my life's journey—the sign saying: Now Entering Texas. Consequently, I was finally leaving Oklahoma after 255 miles of enduring the battery of the winter elements. It's almost mentally overwhelming to experience the phenomenon of sealing your fate from your past, yet it's invigorating at the same time to realize making this much progress of this distance gave me more motivation—injected as a natural stimulant with the cold air rushing through my nose.

CHAPTER 2

LEAVING MY SWEETHEART BEHIND

It was very sad to think back only five days ago and realize that I had left my beautiful high school sweetheart, Mary Ann, back in our hometown. I recalled that she was so peachy sweet with cutesy blonde hair and blue eyes. I remembered standing in her driveway after a date on a hot summer's night. When our eyes met, we were magnetized as my heartstrings were pulled toward her, closer and closer, into embracing with her body close to mine, drawing our lips together, yearning for her sensual wet kiss to take over, melting all of my masculine desires to love her and to someday become intimate. Would she at some time in the future make romance come true? The endorphins raced wildly for her, while we were both trying to figure out, for the first time in our lives, was this what true love felt like? Ah yes! We wanted to find out more and go deeper.

My fantasies were propelling me more now as I was riding the bike just thinking about her, displacing my thoughts about tired thigh muscles. Sweet thoughts can really put a smile on your face, causing people passing by to think, "He looks so elated, yet peddling so hard to try and gain speed. How can he be so happy and enjoy a trip like that?" I learned not to worry about what other people thought about me and enjoyed the elation of thoughts.

Coming upon Shamrock, Texas, I saw a prospective drive-in diner with carport coverings to sleep under. I wondered what the weather might do overnight. This spot looked pretty tempting since I got snow plastered the night before and woke up zombied out. It looked like there were no customers and no open signs. Their parking lot was covered with a layer of snow showing no tracks, making it look deserted, which provoked me to slip and slide my way in to become their overnight customer. It was so cold that the moisture froze on my upper lip. I popped open a can of Vienna sausages, opened some crackers, added some cheese, and gobbled it all down. To shield myself from the shivering cold, I curled up inside my sleeping bag like a caterpillar in a cocoon. Doing this gave me a needed deep sleep without a peep.

With the fear of getting caught, my mind seemed to have been programmed for waking up at a time just before sunrise. Since I was trespassing at the drive-in, I didn't want to get caught sleeping there without permission. In order to make a quick getaway and have breakfast at the same time, I grabbed an apple with my left hand, a banana in the right hand and jumped on my bike and jetted off to start another full day of riding.

Early morning starts were the requirements to make up for loss in traction, slowness of the snow and ice, along with the wind impeding momentum. Freshness of a new day sprang forth with the thrill of the unexpected and seeing everything for the first time in my life. I could not have ever imagined that the almost unbearable conditions to push through were the actual catalyst that dared me to launch out onto the wings of excitement. Now I'd learned a fact of life, through the experience of why people use the phrase "do or die." The thrill of their vision is so strong inside that their bravery pushes them beyond the fear of losing their lives. It's crazy. In some circumstances, the accomplishment makes them the person they want to be. The previous old person in them dies out and a new person emerges with newfound traits. Fear leaves you when courage wells up inside of you to force you to try and succeed, whether you win or lose.

The snow had started falling again from an overcast sky of solid gray clouds trying to hide a bashful sun in a brisk wind, blowing flakes into my face, stinging my eyes like ice darts. I tried pulling my sweater cap down past my eyebrows to lessen the irritation, as it aggravated my will power. Suddenly, a blaring horn shocked me into a swerve to the outside of the road as the driver was losing control, which forced me to dive off to the side, falling facedown, thinking I was going to die. The heavier snow coverage had made me lose proximity of the edge line, and the driver must have thought he was going to nail me—making me a biker trophy on the front of his car. This was not fun! I could have been dead at eighteen with no future life. I picked myself up, assessed if there was any damage to my bicycle, and brushed the snow off me and the bike, to get back on the road again.

Here I am halting progress for a map adjustment and
restart before freezing in place.

The miles of battling the snow blizzard were becoming so very long, concurrent with the monstrous winds devouring the hours, limiting the day. Obviously, there was about as much of a chance to set a long-distance record as a snail's odds to win a race against a rabbit. Ironically, I felt pretty close to the snail's pace, and there were no other options here any time soon.

Being frozen, looking like Frosty the Iceman, with ice on my eyebrows and snowflakes sticking to my chin, I exhausted myself by carrying more frozen water weight than ever before. The bike's narrow street tires were losing so much in traction, again spinning out, it was eroding my confidence to continue. "What if I had slid off into a deep ditch or the side of a hill?" I thought. "Is there a deep enough accumulation to entomb me and hide me until spring? Would anyone ever find me?"

The day drew dark and dreary, with time fleeting quickly. I knew I either had to roll out the sleeping bag on top of the wide-open field or be forced to stop due to darkness or I'd crash into something. I think my mind went crazy, because I wouldn't let the force stop me. I was driven to find any kind of shelter out of desperation, or was it the fact my brain was going numb from the freezing wind? I didn't know if anything was out there, being that the Texas Panhandle looked pretty desolate.

In the distance, three little dots came up. Would this be an imaginary disappointment, or could this be something to help me to survive?

As I pedaled closer, the first dot was a little sign saying "Black Texas," not even on the map. At this point, I'd take anything I could. Continuing to pump hard to get closer to the next two dots, I saw that one dot was a grain elevator and the other was a small convenience store with two gas pumps. This seemed like a lifeline that could save me from drowning. I was robbed of motivation to continue and more hungry than a starved, crazed wild cat.

I rolled up to the side of the entry door, leaned my bike up against the side of the building, and sought out some food.

I was greeted by a middle-aged husky-looking man asking, "Where are you going on that bike?"

"All the way to California to join the Marine Corps," I replied.

"You've got to be crazy, trying to ride a bike like that in all of this snow! You should just take a bus or drive a car out there!"

"Naw! That's just too easy," I replied.

"Well, good luck," he said.

I was about ready to eat anything in sight. So I asked, "Hey man, where are your Hostess Twinkies? I'm starved!"

"Over there on the back shelf," he responded as he pointed.

I eagerly bought four packages for my dinner and then I asked him, "Is that little house at the base of the grain elevator like a big dog house?"

He said, "No, that's a water pump shed that keeps the pipes and pump from freezing up."

I said, "Hey! Could I ask you for a favor to help me keep from freezing by staying in there tonight?"

He said, "Sure!"

I thought to myself, "Wow!" This will be like having a room in the Holiday Inn compared to the roughing-it-in-wilderness conditions I had been encountering. After paying for the Hostess Twinkies, I swiped them off the counter as I said, "Thanks a lot!" with the biggest smile on my face since all the nights I'd been sleeping in the cold and snow.

I scurried off to the pump shed, finding the door big enough to roll my bike into. I discovered hay covering the ground as if he had kept animals inside for protection at some time from inclement weather. Being close to Christmas, it made me think of the nativity scenes with Baby Jesus lying in a manger. I started missing being home with my mom, dad, sister Sheila and our dog named Bow for the Christmas celebrations. I realized that I was never again going to experience Christmas with my family while being a teenager for the rest of my life.

As I unrolled the sleeping bag next to a pump motor with a light bulb on it for freeze prevention, I was breathing a sigh of relief, at least for one night not having to fear how cold it was going to get or how deep it would snow on top of me while sleeping. Now I was ready to sit on top of my sleeping bag, with the packages of Twinkies being eyed as my prize for the whole day of hard riding. I was so starved that I tore into the wrapping and devoured them like attacking piranhas. I even licked up every sign of icing and crumbs off the wrappers.

As I relished the sweetness still on the tip of my tongue, I viewed the map and spotted Lubbock, Texas, just about 120 miles south from Black Texas. I remembered how our families had one of the best Christmas gatherings when I was nine years old with Grandpa, Grandma, three aunts and uncles with three cousins in each family. Grandpa and Grandma ran a motel, so they were able to put all of our four families into separate motel units on Christmas Eve night. The grand finale was gathering inside their manager's office to exchange gifts during the evening. For the girl cousins, the dolls were flying out of their wrappings like jack-in-the-boxes with shouts of glee. My cousin Chad got the biggest self-propelled engine train ever seen. It stood as high as my kneecaps with every color of light imaginable, and it made the choo-choo sound as it drove around until it hit something and would automatically reverse and go a new direction.

My older cousin, Larry, got a BB gun—"Don't shoot your eye out," we thought from the movie *A Christmas Story.* I think he was destined to be a soldier because he liked playing Cowboys and Indians.

I was ecstatic when I got my first slot car racing track. We put it together and raced all night with the little headlights on and going pedal to the metal. I was so excited about racing against my sister late into the night that I couldn't stop to get to bed, so Dad had to force the Checker Flag by ripping off a bed sheet, waving it overhead, and covering the whole race track. Dad said, "You're not racing all night! Now get into bed."

The whole family had been so caught up in such a heavenly celebration, with everyone laughing to their hearts content, that I wished that every Christmas could be like that. Unfortunately, it was probably the only one, never to be outdone again.

The sugar infusion kept me racing back into all of the memories, but it was getting late in the shed. The reality of needing sleep to restore my energy for tomorrow's long battle back into the weather elements convinced me to quickly dose off to dream land.

CHAPTER 3

A PAUPER
AT A KING'S TABLE

Morning came with the ease of packing up in dryer, warmer conditions. I rolled my bike back over to the front of the store, thinking I had to buy more Hostess Twinkies to survive the next 45 to 75 miles.

After I came through the front door, the husky storeowner yelled across the store at me, saying, "Young man, come over here. I want to show you something." He opened the doorway curtains that separated the store side from his actual living quarters and then—WOW! I stepped across the threshold of his dining room with the table covered with the most eye-popping, sensational six-course breakfast I'd ever seen.

Then a beautiful young girl of about seventeen was standing beside the table. She seemed to have dropped down out of a dream. My jaw also dropped in elation and in attraction to her, as she danced around the table with her voluptuous smile, describing each dish she had prepared. Truly, she was the most beautiful "Hostess with the Mostess" in all of Texas ever before. She said, "Well, my name is Julie."

I said, "I'm Daniel."

"Nice to meet you," she said.

"Did you fix all of this yourself?" I asked.

She replied, "Yes, especially for you, as our guest. We wanted to invite you to join us."

I thought, "How could I refuse?"

The store owner said, "Well, come on, sit down with us. Don't be so goggle-eyed."

I couldn't pry my eyes from her and obeyed his order to take a chair, feeling like a pauper at a king's table of royalty.

He shared that he was a widower, having lost his wife in a horrific car crash, had no family, and was making a living by running this store. He had hired Julie from Amarillo to help keep house, plan meals, and keep him company. She had the face of an angel with enticing big brown eyes, wavy brown hair, with a sexy model-like figure. My inner thoughts were to break out of my shyness to propose to be her man and abandon my goals to bike to California. After all, isn't life about meeting the girl of your dreams, marrying her, having kids, earning lots of money, owning a big house, and living happily ever after? Well, she could definitely have made me feel like the happiest man in the whole wide world forever. Especially with Julie's words of kindness commending me for trying to make such an impossible journey of a lifetime and having bravery. She had given me a new motivation not to quit. I was caught up in her charming smile making me feel fluttery, as if I had butterflies in my stomach. At the same time my taste buds were turning flips over the delightful breakfast.

A surprise act of kindness from a king and the warmth of a princess touched me greatly. This was one of the most treasured experiences that I had ever known. She wrapped up some boiled eggs and biscuits for my lunch to take with me on the road. They gave me their hearts of compassion, when I had nothing to give in return for my appreciation but a smile and expressions of happiness. It meant a lot to me just to give them a simple hand shake. The three of us were in mutual enjoyment of this unique morning and making a memory we would have for the rest of our lives. This was goodbye forever, however. As I walked toward my bike, looking back, they both stood at the door and waved, elevating me to a status of an "Iron Man."

Then I mounted my trusty steed, turning my face toward the West, with the reality of the piercing cold wind bursting my bubble, destroying my dream-like euphoria and making me reluctantly awake.

I had to return to my committed vision of what I must do: No matter what it would take, even if it turned crazy out there, with a crash and burn. The hearty breakfast of royalty had inflated my ego to the point that I felt invincible and driven, even with the tires sliding around out of control. The bitter cold of the morning kept most living creatures in a holding pattern inside any kind of shelter.

The cold snow triggered my remembrance of my big white boxer named Butch that I once took to a snow-covered park. He pranced out in front of me to give me a tow on my sled like a team of sled dogs. This actually happened when I was eleven, running in Turner Park, in Tulsa. Butch, whom we got from my aunt and uncle in Lubbock, Texas, had come up beside me and pulled the rope out of my hand to pull me through the snow on my sled. Some dogs must have an inherent ability, generated by the friskiness of the cold, to pull and run for fun. Butch was in a tug-of-war mindset and would growl with a series of barks through his clenched teeth clamped down on the rope. With his powerful strut like a stallion, I hung on tight to stay on the sled as I marveled at his out-of-control will to pull me clear to the next town if no one stopped him. I got a taste of dog sled racing that day.

I set my sights on the possibility of making it to Clovis, New Mexico, because I have another aunt, uncle, and three cousins there. I decided to take the time and go the additional mileage to venture off Route 66 and take Highways 87 and 60 to get there.

This was taking me farther south and the sun was starting to show through the clouds, bringing rays of welcomed warmth. The snow-packed roads were becoming slushy and mushy, making for a wet spin-off from my tires onto my legs. My boots kept me from getting wet feet and helped maintain traction on my pedals, but the shins of my legs were wet and cold. I was becoming more excited at the thought of being so close to making it to Clovis, and I began looking at this like completing a long-distance race with arriving in the driveway and breaking the ribbon in first place. I could see their faces now, beaming with congratulatory smiles, open arms, and cameras rolling. Setting a record of pedaling a bike 450 miles in the snow, going from Tulsa to Clovis in 9 days.

Well, rolling into my aunt and uncle's driveway wasn't quite that rewarding, but they were excited to see me. It was also a relief to have made it for the purpose of washing my clothes and sleeping bag and getting rest.

After all of these years of driving to Clovis for Christmas with my dad, mom, and sister to be greeted by two to four sets of other family members, it was quite a different picture. In fact, the reality of my arrival was a lot less dramatic, with more of a surprised look when my aunt answered the door. The appearance of my aunt was the confirmation that I really had to reconnect with her, for my own peace of mind.

She said, "I just can't believe you're here on a bicycle by yourself. Well, come on in! I bet you're totally exhausted and starved."

I responded, saying, "Yeah, I've pushed myself to really make it here to see you all one last time before I pursue my journey to San Diego and go into the Marine Corps. Hopefully, no 'crash and burns' will happen and completing the 1500 miles will qualify me, in my way of thinking, into acceptance by the military."

My aunt had a way of speaking her mind in what she thought was witty but not quite tactful. She just had to say, "My lands, what kind of craziness are you doing, riding a bike when you could be just as qualified getting there in a car? Are they giving you any kind of medal for it?"

"Naw!"

Uncle Bill had to say, "Well, he's doing it his way! It's going to be more notable and less crazy than you think."

Well, we had to bring up the past year's traditions of gathering around the dinner table for Uno, Yahtzee, other card games, and to talk about funny times throughout our lives.

As Aunt Glenda cooked up a dinner for us, I completely overloaded her washing machine with all that I had. After all of those days and miles out on the road, I probably smelled like an old bear wallowing in a stinky, muddy, swamp patch, so I didn't have to beg to use the shower. I felt like layers of sweat and dirt had to be scraped off as I reunited my body to what I had missed for so long. A nice hot shower never felt so good! Ah! I felt like a new man. I must have been suspended in time for about an hour. Aunt Glenda had to convince me, since I had spent such a long time in the restroom, that they were going to have to call in a missing persons report and that I would miss dinner. That got my attention. One starving maniac prepared to charge the dinner table. My appetite was quickly greeted by the aroma of a well-seasoned and breaded chicken fried steak. Oh boy! I was salivating before I could even sit down. They seated me at the head of the table as their star guest of the year. I really had not anticipated the special treatment that they gave me. It was as if I were one of their long-lost sons.

Uncle Bill shared about his highway construction projects, as he operated the giant road graders, skip loaders, and other heavy equipment. With him driving the big trucks and taking command of the massive machinery, he probably felt like his company exalted him to be King of the Road. Uncle Bill loved his job and stated, "Just give me a thermos jug of coffee, warm coat, gloves, and an on-board stereo system, and I'll be on top of the world in the big rigs."

Well, then it was time to help clear off the table, pull out the spare room sleeper sofa bed that I remembered from past years of spending the nights with my cousins, Chad and Kevin, when we were kids, having tickling matches and laughing until we giggled ourselves into trouble, keeping everyone else awake. These were usually times like Thanksgiving Eves or Christmas Eves, having such wonderful fun being together. But for tonight, just a solid solo sleep was what I needed.

Mornings around the Fishers' house always came early because of Uncle Bill's highway construction work. I think they had a rooster for that reason of getting everyone going early, way before the alarm clocks were set to go off. That started a chain reaction, causing the dogs to start barking. The smell of coffee percolating, the crackle of the bacon and eggs frying on the stove top and the aroma of biscuits in the oven all drew me into the kitchen, with the dogs barking for samples before the food could reach the breakfast table. It was quite a chaotic atmosphere. No one ever slept late around here!

After breakfast and everyone had given me good luck wishes as they left for work or school, I got packed up and prepared the bike for launching off for the next 1050 miles on Highway 60. This was a lot better outlook, with the sun shining bright and clear skies to really spark my eagerness to hit the road. I was further charged-up by the lifting-up of what seemed like sponsorship support from the family. I was heading west through the snow melting from the direct sunrays, and I was seeing what could be the best road conditions since riding in mostly snow blizzard conditions from Tulsa. I was setting my sights on making this day's trip of 55 miles to Fort Summer, New Mexico. It was quite assuring, when I did my multiple-point mechanical check on the bike that it boosted my confidence to feel invincible. Then, all of a sudden, the remnants of a snow clump hid a large rock that I hit, twisted my steering. The cold air gave me an alertness to quickly catch myself by putting my foot down and recovering before wiping out, as I was keeping forward momentum. I was not going to fret over a little spilt milk. Onward, without another thought of road hazards throwing me into the ditch.

CHAPTER 4

THE INFAMOUS
BILLY THE KID

Coming into the Fort Summer city limits, I was looking for signs of buildings or military installations, but it was nothing like I imagined. After all, why did they call the town a fort if they didn't have tanks, heavy artillery, soldiers and fortifications? But, I guess the actual fort was probably in a more secluded, preserved area of history. There was a surprising sign saying, HOME OF BILLY THE KID, which we never learned that much about from any of our books back home. Wow! I actually rode my bike where Billy the Kid rode his horse! He was one of the fastest gunslingers in the West. Whipping out his guns with bullets flying, racing his horse through town and being a holy terror and winner of all of the gun fights.

I was transported back in time, envisioning what it was like to exist as a cowboy. The ruggedness of surviving the outdoor wilderness, beasts, and finding food and water. Sometimes life would be seen as kill or be killed. Even now, I could be seen as a vulnerable target, carrying lots of loot, but I didn't think to carry a gun to protect myself.

Men had to build their own shelters without precut materials and had very few supplies or tools, with no construction companies in existence then. It was a wonder that they lived through that era of time without losing more lives, or how they even started these small towns in the middle of nowhere.

And this was what you call the flatlands. From Fort Summer to Yeso, Vaughn, Encino and up to Clines Corner. It's like "A Thousand Miles from Nowhere." They made a song with that title. Some of these little towns only have a few buildings, and no one around with dark overcast skies makes them look like ghost towns. The spookiness drove me to peddle faster to find roadside tables on which to sleep. Between Yeso and Vaughn, one saw tons of cactuses, tumble weeds and desert-like terrain.

I thank my dad for teaching me to fix things in the garage, which played a big part in my ability to take care of breakdowns on the road, even though I was riding a French-made Jeunet 10-speed. Fixing flat tires, pumping more air into the tires, and adjusting components were always imperative demands to keep me going. However, after pushing the bike hard all the way through Oklahoma, Texas, and part of the way in New Mexico, the rear wheel was finally giving out. There are some things you just can't fix on the roadside, for instance, the rear wheel breaking a lot of spokes on the gear cluster side. Due to the weight of all my luggage and rough roads, the spokes snapped off and could not be threaded through the axle hub to the rim without having a special gear cluster tool. I wasn't prepared to handle this. So, the dreaded nightmare of literally being stopped in my tracks was about to happen to me any moment now. What this meant was that the back tire wobbled from side to side, rubbing the inside of the frame tubes, like holding the brakes on tight while trying to pedal.

Coming from Clines Corner with a brisk wind chill factor close to twenty degrees caused me to try to cover my face more with no relief. Brrr! The back wheel was trying to freeze up, scraping the inside of the bike frame. If it totally stopped and it kept me from pedaling, my goose would be cooked—it would be all over, and I could just freeze to death out here or hope that some passerby could haul me in to find any kind of shelter available. Dreading the thought of this dilemma ever possibly happening, I pumped harder and harder, without a solution. What did you do when a wheel completely jammed? I didn't know! I guess I failed. Like if a mountain climber's hooks or ropes break—he dies.

My entire 1500-mile quest would have ended up in the headlines of the newspaper saying: EIGHTEEN-YEAR-OLD CYCLIST FOUND DEAD BESIDE THE ROAD BELIEVED TO BE ATTEMPTING TO SET A LONG-DISTANCE RECORD RIDE FROM TULSA, OKLAHOMA, TO SAN DIEGO, CALIFORNIA. The investigation on the bike would reveal that the extremely frigid temperatures had frozen up the wheels, causing the rider to skid off into a snow-packed ditch. The autopsy would have indicated that he was frozen stiff as a board, as no one discovered him for days.

I thought to myself, "Gosh! I have to keep on pushing. I can't stop for anything!" I was exerting every ounce of energy to try and make it to Albuquerque, where maybe I had a better chance to be rescued. This had become a panicky time of riding, pleading in my spirit that the rear wheel would hold up and crying silently inside for help.

Then a completely unplanned surprise just came in sight at the perfect time—a bike shop business was just up ahead, to the left of the highway. After the bike almost seized up, I pushed it through the front door with a desperate search for someone to greet me.

The owner of the shop, a neatly trimmed Latino guy, approached me, asking, "Whoa, man! Can I help you?"

I responded, "You won't believe this, I've come all the way from Tulsa, Oklahoma, but within the last 100 miles or so, my back tire has been trying to seize up by hitting the inside of the frame. It's because of so many broken spokes that I can't replace because of a special sprocket gear tool that's needed. Can you let me borrow one to take it off and thread new spokes in?"

He said, "Sure, man, I'll even help you get your bike on a bike stand and let you get started. We will be glad to help you out any way we can, and don't worry about paying us anything."

WOW! I felt like a beggar off the street, begging for mercy, and then all of a sudden, I was brought into being honored and sponsored like a world competitor on the front center stage.

I proceeded to loosen the axle nuts and unchain the sprockets, in order to fit the special sprocket gear tool, which removed it. This was a perfect match, and it came off like clockwork. Next I removed all of the broken spokes and threaded in new ones. After that came putting the wheel on a "truing fork," which held the wheel steady while I tightened the spokes on the appropriate side to pull the rim into alignment. I used aircraft wire to tie the cross of the spokes tightly for reinforcement. After truing the wheel, replacing the tube protector, tube, tire, and airing them up at the proper pressure, the repairs were completed.

I discovered that there are truly some very good people in this world who want to give graciously and care for others without asking for anything in return. In a way, this Latino guy and the Albuquerque Bike Shop crew were supporting me, believing that this was the most important repair made on the bike in order to make it more possible for me to reach the coast of California, unless misfortune took its course.

All of the bike shop personnel seemed happy for me, as their smiles had the effect of a pat on the back and wishing me good luck, wanting me to make it all the way.

It was nearing the end of the day as the owner informed me of the record below-freezing forecast for that night to drop down to single digits and -7 degree wind chill. He gave me directions to a homeless shelter for a warm shower, dinner, and a warm bed. This sounded too good to be true, but I rolled out his front door into the already shocking 15 degrees, convincing me to pursue this detour to find the shelter.

I found the Albuquerque Men's Homeless Shelter, wondering how I would be able to park my bike in a safe area. One of the worst tragedies would be getting my rebuilt bike and all of my belongings stolen. I'd be severed from my lifeline to go one more inch toward my destination without my bike—which had been like a buddy to me. After all, this was one of the worst neighborhoods in town of the down-and-out—desperate men, maybe stealing to buy liquor, clothes, or food.

My worries subsided when the housekeeper allowed me to roll my bike into a room and lay it against the wall beside one of the many bunk beds inside this huge house. I couldn't believe it could come about to have this homeless shelter available, right on the very night of the worst freeze in history and just when my bike was breaking down on the road earlier in the day, before discovering the bike shop.

Showering in hot water definitely beat staying out on the road risking becoming a frozen stiff. The food servers were like lifesavers, knowing that they were gladly giving us a hot meal of roast beef, potatoes, and bread to live on because most of us were on the verge of starvation. Even as poor as I was, having nothing to give to these other men and not knowing how I'd find food for the upcoming trip, I had a sense of humbleness, seeing these other men around me being destitute, homeless and broke. What gave me hope with virtual fortitude was that at least I was young and going somewhere to find a purpose in life. All of these men looked like they had lost their purpose in life from some failures or misfortune that happened to them.

I came back to my bottom bunk, hungrily wolfing down my plate of food faster than a mighty shop vacuum. I got up to dispose of my plate and brush my teeth. Then, upon coming back to my bottom bunk, I saw an older man had stolen it away from me. I said, "Excuse me, sir, this is my bunk bed, can't you see my bike leaning on the wall beside my bed?"

He said, "No, I slept here last night, this my bed, you varmint! Older men get the bottom bunks and younger ones have to take the top bunks."

Well, I thought in my mind, just wait a minute here, who made up that rule, and I was not going to let an old scuzzy man push me around. So told him, "That doesn't sound right, the housekeeper said that I can put my bike there and that's the bed he knew I would take."

He kicked me in the leg, and I grabbed my tote bag and whopped him in the head. Then the whole room of guys started going crazy, attacking us by beating us with pillows. Complete chaos had broke out, which caused the housekeeper to come in and yell out, "Break it up, or I'll throw you all out into the cold."

I explained the whole thing and he settled it by telling the older man to sleep in a different room. We definitely didn't want to give up our Holiday Inn accommodations for duking it out or let our differences cause us to regret it by learning a hard cold lesson. Well, when all the pillows were back on the beds, we had a lot of respect for our privilege to be accepted here and jumped into the bunk beds eagerly. I clutched the top of the blankets to pull them down, immediately taking possession. Lights went out in our room, but the nearby window appeared as if someone had turned a light switch on outside. Amazingly the full moon behind the winter lining of clouds had illuminated the whole sky, and what snow covering there was actually reflected everywhere so you could see pretty good outside. I had to pull the covers over my head to get the night effect and dose off to wonderland.

There was a rumble, I fell out of the bed, and all of a sudden I felt something pulling at me and there was a shake from a hooded figure to get my attention, then a whisper from someone unknown in the dark of the night, saying, "Don't make any noise, I have something to show you, come with me." I could not recognize his disguised voice. He helped pull me up off the floor, taking me by the arm to hold onto them, causing me to feel compelled in a mysterious way to yield to their invitation. My first inclination was to ask where we were going, but others were asleep around us and so I didn't talk. I was being led with a small penlight into further darkness to somewhere only this person knew to go, and I had to trust his direction. There seemed to be a maze of various hallways, until his penlight was pointed to shine upon a half door, opening into a set of stairs going to a basement. Then he whispered again, "Shut the door quietly behind you and come down the stairs with me."

I was curious who this was and why they were leading me downstairs. We reached the bottom, and a dim black light came on. I asked, "Who are you, and what are trying to show me?"

As the person slipped off their hood, I started seeing blond hair fall out and completely surprise me—this was not a man, but a young girl my age—it was Mary Ann, my sweetheart who I left in Tulsa.

We instantly reached out to each other, wrapping our arms around in a tight embrace with her smiling sweet lips meeting mine with a sweet juicy wet kiss, engaging ourselves in the long-awaited romance we desired, as with two lovers wanting to make each other happy in love. She sent me into an excited frenzy, guiding me over to her bed and causing me to roll onto it with our bodies so magnetized together. Our emotional high was so intertwined, triggering our sensual desire to fulfill each other. She had me so turned on, I couldn't resist. She started unbuttoning her blouse, showing her cleavage.

Then BAM! I got slapped in the face. WHAT HAPPENED? Oh no, it was not Mary Ann's hand, it was a rude awakening of the housekeeper's hand trying to get me out of the bunk bed. "Get up, get up!" he shouted. "Time for breakfast!" I had just been reluctantly forced from a dream of ecstasy back into a cold reality.

Having no choice, I rolled out of bed and slowly stumbled to the dining room. I moped while eating a hot bowl of oatmeal, being disappointed over losing the most real, euphoric dream I've ever had. This was the quickest encounter of emotional excitement that I had ever experienced in a dream. It was as if someone had pressed a button to cause a fantasy to happen, then they pressed another button to deflate my passion. Have you ever had a dream where you wished that you had stayed asleep long enough to find out what would have happened? Maybe the dream will be repeated or continue on a night in the future. But if not, we can always choose to let our imagination go wild.

The one consolation of this morning was a hot breakfast, and it was free! This homeless shelter definitely had been a lifesaver, helping me to survive.

After brushing my teeth, packing all my belongings, and checking the luggage bags to be strapped on tight, I started rolling my bike toward the front door. The housekeeper greeted me with a line of questioning, saying, "I usually ask everyone a few questions before they leave, like, "are you coming back tonight, but with you having a bike packed up like that, I guess you've got places you're going?"

I answered back with, "Yep, going all the way to California to join the Marine Corps."

The housekeeper said, "Wow! How are you getting food to eat without money?"

I replied, "I'm not sure! Maybe my Dad can wire funds or people will help me out."

The housekeeper asked, "Were you happy with your bed and meals here?"

I replied, "I really couldn't ask for more, and I was so glad you were here for me—so far away from home."

With the housekeeper breaking a smile on his face, he concluded his questioning by saying, "Adios and happy trails."

I pulled my warm coat, cap, and gloves on, trying to brace myself for the seventeen-degree morning air, and then headed down the sidewalk to the street connecting back to the Interstate 40 and Route 66.

CHAPTER 5

SURPRISE STOP BY THE POLICE

The bitter cold forced me to pedal more rapidly to try to stay warm and made me more aggressive to pursue the progress toward California. At least it was warming to see the bright yellow sunbeams glance off the refrozen water crystals over the surface of the snow. I set my sights on reaching Casa Blanca, which was about 55 miles away. If the road conditions permitted, I planned on surging ahead faster to help make up for the extra time it took to repair my bike. I couldn't find a separate path from Route 66, so the only way to get through the towns going west was to actually enter onto and travel Interstate 40. These were great roads with wide shoulders to ride on for clear sailing ahead.

I was just "cadillacing along," when all of a sudden there were sirens and flashing lights out of nowhere. I looked behind me to see that a New Mexico police car was pulling me over as if I were an escaped convict. The officer explained there were no bikes or pedestrians allowed on Interstate 40 within the city limits. He said he'd have to fine me $50.00 and that I must follow him to the police station to pay up.

When we arrived at the police station, I explained that I couldn't find any other highway other than detouring over 100 miles out of my way down to Highway 60. I told them I didn't have the money. The patrol officer said, well we could throw you in jail for a couple of days. The only thing I knew to do was explain to them that I was going into the Marine Corps and I had to be there by the deadline. Then I thought, *maybe I should call Dad to have him wire over the money to pay the fine.* The clerk was satisfied with that and was convinced to release me from the police station. I was so relieved because that could have given me a police record and I might not have made it to San Diego on time.

I had to travel on frontage roads and side streets until I got out of town. After not seeing a police car for miles, I tried to sneak back onto Interstate 40 and make a fast getaway. I felt like I was going over the minimum 40 mph, as if I were a getaway driver after a bank robbery. After pedaling a couple miles of seeing less civilization and more country, I started breathing a sigh of relief. My unexpected brush with the law caused a hurdle that I had to overcome. It caused more wasted time, and I had to push faster now to make it up. I popped out an apple to chomp on for lunch and gulped fast sips of water to stay on the go. The day passed so quickly from my motivated getaway as I fled from the police station. I managed to cover another 45 miles, which drew me closer to California.

Watching the blowing tumbleweeds in the cold amber sunset signaled that I was back on a roll again and, also that I was aloft and lost in time. It was funny how fast and effortlessly the tumbleweeds were going, and yet with my racing determination, they were outrunning me. Darkness forced me to unroll my sleeping bag in a roadside clearing where a smooth round rock would be my pillow. I was going off into la-la land with a nippy whistling wind sounding kind of scary with it being so lonely. Pulling my head inside the bag was instant security for dozing off. Night passed quickly in a blink of an eye, and boom! There was light, and I was eager to spring into flight!

Seeing the rising sun or seeing the snow clouds glowing in the early morning was my alarm clock throughout my journey. I just never thought that I would sleep late or not having of an alarm clock would cause me to run late for the deadline. My mindset adjusted to the early turn-in at sunset with the need to regenerate through early sleep so that I could more easily arise rested and ready to go.

I failed to reach Casa Blanca before dark last night,because of the time it took being forced to go to the police station, so I decided to pack fast and ride into town for breakfast. Just a couple of eggs, toast, bacon and orange juice would be my fuel for the day. Fast in and out to get back on the pathway to make it to Gallup.

My Uncle Bill had mentioned that I should plan to stop at an address he gave me to visit his mother, just half a mile off the highway, and tell her about my expedition. Mrs. Fisher's house was easy to find on the corner. It was very small with white hardwood siding that was just a "plain Jane" style.

I knocked on the door and surprised her: "Hi, Mrs. Fisher, I'm Daniel, Uncle Bill's nephew."

"Oh yes," she said, "he called and told me you were coming, but that was a while back, you know! I didn't know if you got caught by coyotes or you sailed straight through, going with the wind, ha ha! Well, you know! I am glad you found my address, so come on in."

She was kind of a funny character, laughing and saying, "you know" all the time. I figured she was doing that out of habit instead of possibly making fun of people. She was being witty at times by saying things like, "Are you shy, or did the cat get your tongue?"

She offered me dinner and I thought, "How could I refuse?" As she was fixing our meals, she invited me to look through all of the many family pictures on all of the shelves. Wow! There was Uncle Bill in uniform when he served in the Army during WWII. It appeared that his training in the service gave him the skills to operate heavy equipment, tanks, deuce and a half trucks in civilian life and handle any of the giant highway construction equipment.

She served up our dinners on her very quaint yellow painted table. As we started eating, Mrs. Fisher became a historian, telling me all about Uncle Bill's growing up years and what it was like walking in his shoes.

After this great home-cooked meal, I looked outside. Seeing at least three more hours of daylight left, I decided to catch up on lost time and try to make it to the Arizona border line—escaping the New Mexico police. Then I'd have to discover if the Arizona highways have those overly strict "No Scooters, Bicycles or Pedestrian" signs. It was just crazy—you could see they put in new highways with wide shoulders in places where there was plenty of room for riding on the shoulder (wider than a car). Then we couldn't use them. Shoot! Most of the highways I had traveled across Oklahoma, Texas, and some in New Mexico had no shoulders. They just had about 12 inches for marking the outside line. This brought to my remembrance the songs like "I Walk the Line," since I realized I had been riding the line for hundreds of miles, and the song by Leon Russell saying, "I'm up on the tight wire, one side's ice and one is fire." Well, for me to go a little too far on either side was going to look pretty ugly. It was really a narrow margin of survival.

As I rode like I was in the last mile of a 20-mile race to reach the finish line, the roads ahead of me were following the sun going down. With the bright colors of orange glancing off the surface— I could have started singing, "Follow the Yellow Brick Road," but the exertion of my determination to cross over the Arizona border zapped my singing voice.

Chasing the sun before it went below the horizon and looking ahead to where I would sleep was my present quest. Just passing the "Now Entering Arizona" sign, I breathed a little easier and scoped out a resting place. I saw a little sign coming up and it read, "Little Town but Big Hearts. Lupton, Population: ten." What looked like a little white cone from a distance, as I got closer to see it better, turned out to be a big teepee. It was like a little convenience store. I saw an Indian behind the counter, who said, "I'm Engine Joe."

Then I said "Hi. Wow! This is the biggest teepee I've ever seen in my life. How many people did it take to build this?"

He said, "All ten of us, and tons of wooden posts. Are you traveling far?"

I replied, "Yes! But, not tonight because I don't have any lights, but in the morning I'll set my sights on California. Would you mind if I stay inside to sleep and keep warm?"

He said, "Not really, but not in big teepee! You must stay in little teepee in back!"

I asked, "How much does that cost?"

He said, "You be our guest."

"Oh thank you so much, Mr. Engine Joe." As I walked behind him to show me the way, I thought, *Yeah! People here really do have big hearts!* I rolled out my sleeping bag for warmth inside and quickly dozed off.

The next morning, my instinctive body alarm clock triggered me to arise to the new day outside the dark covering of the teepee, where I was sleeping. Mr. Engine Joe walked over to open my door flap, found me awake, and promptly invited me into the big teepee again to share in his potato patty and cactus water breakfast. This was a most unusual kind of breakfast, but I was grateful and it got me going. How many people in the world ever experience something like this?

I picked up a few pieces of fruit, got water and sunflower seeds to have for the upcoming miles, then tucked them tightly in my carrying bag to ready myself for the departure. I looked back as I rolled out onto the roadway and saw Mr. Engine Joe one last time raising his right arm in a "L" shape, which is the Indian hello and goodbye salute, which I acknowledged.

So, I started out in low third gear, with the sun at my back and chasing me, shifting up to tenth gear, pursuing the west horizon at a fast clip, planning on winning the race with the sun to Sun Valley, coincidently where the sun would set in front of me at the end of this day. Interstate 40, in this stretch of highway, the hills and slopes were billboarded with huge vertical slabs of red, orange, yellow, and tan rocks. It was very colorful scenery and neat to ride at a bicycle pace, at about 20 to 30 mph, to really enjoy such a different country. Following the route farther west, I noticed the Arizona map states "Painted Cliffs," which does identify the rocky slabs and mountains to the north and south. The diverse terrain of flatness turned into a lot of hilliness after the town of Sanders and I could see the increase of elevation ahead with pretty large mountains in the distance. This triggered thoughts of both dread and determination, because of the ominous appearance of the uphill battle, to drive harder, confronting me with a mission impossible.

This was also an opportunity of a lifetime, being young, energetic, going off the edge of the cliff and feeling invincible.

The most dramatic change in geography was taking place right before my eyes from the desert sand dunes of West New Mexico, when I looked back, to the viewed of multiple colored rock columns of Arizona, and then many miles ahead into the distance seeing the massive giant mountains.

I was imagining being an explorer coming to a different planet for the first time. Then on this new planet I was looking to discover new life forms. Maybe if it was imaginable, to think of coming in contact with angelic beings of beauty, happiness and love. But for now, the reality was it looked awfully dead out here and I was still more than 470 miles from Death Valley. I doubted to find anything living for as far as I could see. Not even imaginable.

My perception of the world had been so small, compared to what I saw now, and it was overwhelmingly larger than my mind could fathom in about 5 to 15 miles of travel, letting my eyes jet out to over 50 miles of elevated masses. With just this tiny fractional part of the Planet Earth's equator distance of 24,902 miles compared to 65 miles of this 1500-mile attempt of my life's time and travel.

I felt like our lives seem so insignificantly tiny compared to the greater scheme of a gigantic world, to try and discover what was our purpose.

So as the saying goes: "I think I'm getting my money's worth" or "this is more than I bargained for." I chose to stick with the program—trying to make the distance.

After the day's very scenic ride, with clear skies, I saw the big ball of fire starting to land in Sun Valley, which also signaled me to "land this tired body" in a resting place before dark, since I had no lights. I parked the bike and rolled out the sleeping bag quickly to prevent unknowingly going over a cactus or a rattlesnake in the dark.

CHAPTER 6

FUN ON MOTORCYLCES

The squawking of migrating geese overhead performed the awaking alarm to get me going. I knew that I couldn't waste any time, so I chomped down some peanut butter crackers as I was rolling up the sleeping bag. Being deprived of having a shower for many days now, I probably smelled like a barn animal. I just hoped I wouldn't attract any unwanted critters at night. I was now driven to pedal as fast as I could to arrive in Flagstaff, Arizona, which was a little over 100 miles, in order to get a motel to shower. I was glad that I was not going into the public places to encounter people looking at me, asking me if I forgot to use deodorant.

I set my sights on making it to Winslow, Arizona, the half-way point, and to plan a desperate stop in Flagstaff. Now the beautiful mountains were being illuminated by the morning sun and appeared to radiate with warmth and a glow. I was drawn to jetting faster toward the mountain passes, using Interstate 40, it being the only south central-route that's the best and being the gateway to the West.

I discovered along this route of an increasing incline that there were Indian teepees from a civilized tribe as I was pedaling through to Holbrook at an elevation of 5,057 ft. It was amazing that the natives survived in this area without anything around to sustain them, being so desolate from many moons ago. How did they do it? Maybe it was "savage aggression" and "survival of the fittest."

I could have imagined using bow and arrows to snag wild game, but they had been able to bring down buffalo on horseback with spears and find underground streams in dry desert terrain to survive. Come to think of it, if I didn't have my bike to get to the next town that was more than 150 miles apart, which was about three days out for me, or try to walk that far, I probably wouldn't make it because of thirst or starvation. The Indians somehow survived for centuries. This long expedition was forcing the Daniel Boone to come out in me, who was a frontiersman on television for many years. Sometimes being confronted with extreme circumstances in life, makes you do what you have to do, causing you to react instinctively. I look back and know that I never expected to fly through the air with a loaded 10-speed, as I did riding over unexpected humps in the road, going fast downhill. You hold tight and keep your sense of balance to land "rubber side down," or else it could be a pretty bad wipe out.

These risky encounters caused flashbacks of riding my Honda 50 at fourteen years old in the strip pits along Yale Avenue in North Tulsa, which was the most popular off-road hill climbing and rolling hills jumping arena in all of Northeastern

Oklahoma. People came from all around to take to some or all of the challenges involving powering up vertical walls to try and make it to the top. Racing around the scrambles track was where you could reach speeds over 55 m.p.h. But the most popular and daring was the rolling hills racing. Motorcyclists would ride up these hills fast enough to get airborne off the tops, then landing, you were compressing your shocks and flattening your tires completely upon landing. But the greater uncertainty was not knowing if you were going to collide head on with another rider coming from the opposite direction. It was pretty wild! It was exhilarating and caused us to be instant motorcycle stuntmen. I wasn't quite as insane as the big bore riders that almost jumped the whole valley between the hills. As I stayed parked on top of one of the series of seven hills, I could see them come off the tops so high in the air that you knew they were risking their lives. Then on Sunday afternoons, you would see riders do high-speed

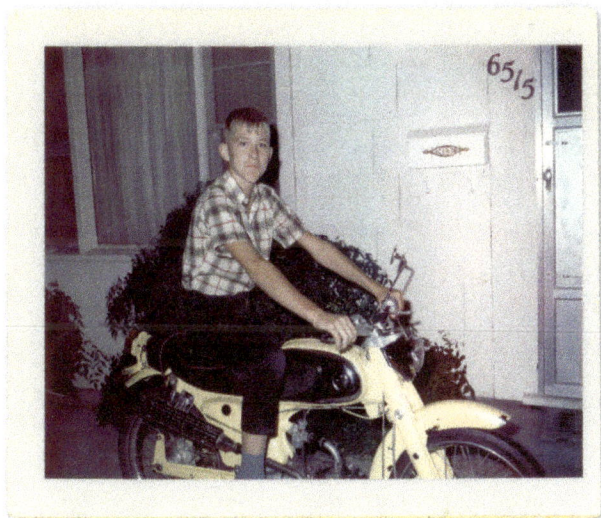

First motorcycle. I was fourteen when I purchased my first Honda 50 motorcycle with the money I saved from working at Kentucky Fried Chicken and delivering newspapers.

wheelies in third and fourth gears on Honda 305 scramblers and Suzuki 400 racers, going down Yale. If the police ever came after them, they would just cut a trail into the strip pits and get away, thinking, "Catch me if you can, but you'll never find me without being on a fast dirt bike!" I tell you, it became so heavily ridden with so many motorcycles that I think the police avoided the area on weekends. This was our ultimate excitement to outdo ourselves or take on a race with whoever showed up. So, I think having some trail riding experience probably helped me in many areas of keeping control of my bike to withstand shaky road conditions.

Now the cold day's windy trail was bringing me into Winslow, Arizona, where the famous Eagles song titled "Take it Easy" was singing about: "Standing on the corner in Winslow, Arizona, It's such a fine sight to see," on this very spot of Route 66.

I never knew about the historical sighting of one of the world's largest meteor craters, which was posted on a sign. Albert E. Foote surveyed the meteor crater in 1897, an actual gigantic meteorite impact from a meteor traveling 40,000 mph, causing a crater 560 ft. deep and 2 ½ miles wide, over 50,000 years ago. Wow! It probably blasted a lot of the dinosaurs off the planet back then.

Winslow also has a recreational Clear Creek Lake, where one does cliff diving and kayaking to enjoy the heat of the summer. Just thinking of soaking up the hot sunrays on the red rocks above the big hot tub of Clear Creek generated warmth for my riding. The irony of being aboard a 10-speed was, I could go through towns, big and small, but not enjoy the high points of places to stop or encounter the experiences by spending time to meet someone or make a significant memory that I would like. So, as visitors and local people saw me peadling along the roadway, they were usually shocked to see a bike so loaded down that it looked as big as a buffalo with wheels strolling along. I could have been the last sighting in the world of this lone biker who could only go so far before being devoured by the weather elements of the depth of winter. I resisted stopping at most of the convenience stores, gas stations, motels, and fascinating places to see, to get to a roadside resting stop or somewhere beyond civilization to sleep overnight.

Before the darkness of the night blinded me and could have taken me hostage to what could be out there, I had spotted a hollowed out part of a big rock that wasn't occupied by any creeping things. So, I made a motel room out of it. At least it offered some protection from some of the cold winds. This was the last sticky night before making it for my long awaited hot shower in a warm motel in Flagstaff. The anticipation was so strong, I was sure that the soothing shower would be in my dreams. There was a whistling wind in the distance with the element of a chill, causing me to cuddle tighter in my sleeping bag. Deeper into the night, far into the rocky hills, I heard yelping and chattering, which I thought was dogs in pain, but later I figured it must have been young coyotes searching for game. It became difficult to fall asleep without any surety of not getting attacked in my sleep, but somehow I conked out, counting sheep, but not the ones being attacked by the coyotes.

Morning came quickly, with a sense of urgency to get to Flagstaff. So, I sprang up like a pogo stick because of the double motivation driving me to accomplish my goal of traveling over three quarters of the total distance, which gave me the feeling of I'm almost there, and I would plan to reward myself with a desperately needed hot shower. Therefore, I wasted no time in throwing the sleeping bag on the back of the seat and setting a charge to go faster than any of my previous recent mornings.

The crisp bright morning sun was stimulating like hot coffee on a drowsy morning. I recounted coming over a thousand miles of having to overcome so many obstacles with just a bicycle and highways to make it all happen. This stretch of highway began with a straight shot to the west, with the sunbeams coming from the east illuminating the first sight of San Francisco Mountain peaks with snowcaps. I estimated them to be probably over 100 miles away, with a vast heavy dark gray blanket of ominous snow clouds above them. These mountains of such awe-inspiring beauty had to have been the biggest and longest range I'd ever seen in my life. I also must say the San Francisco Mountains were some of my journey's best high points. It was said that the Sacred San Francisco Peaks Mountains were referred to in the Navajo language as "Dokooosliid," which means "Where Light Shines from Within." I felt that everyone should see these at least once in his or her lifetime.

The anticipated conditions nearing Flagstaff were likely to be snowy and icy. There was presently a small bare strip of asphalt to ride on, but the terrain on either side of the road had a 2-inch covering of snow with some yucca, cactus, and rocks poking through. It almost seemed decorative, as well as so rustic that a painter could never capture its uniqueness. Yet the earth's entire splendor, to take in the view, didn't cause me to slow down, but instead it excited me to drive faster, as if these things of nature were cheering me on to be first place in this race.

Trying to keep a fast pace with an increase of elevation was wearing me down. I had to pull over to an exposed rock, just high enough to sit on and lean my bike on. Then I grabbed the water bottle to wet my whistle and find my last Hostess Twinkie and apple for lunch.

Feeling a bit more reenergized, I remounted and got back on the pace. After several miles, I noticed the sun caught me from behind, and it was quite a bit past midday. Farther down Route 66 in the distance were two huge leaning poles with big tail fins at the top. OH! As I got closer, they had spear tips in the ground. Now it became obvious what these were—they were two arrows, of course! And as I got close enough, I could see the biggest of the group of white buildings saying, "Twin Arrows Trading Post," which had a gift shop, gas station, mechanic's garage, and a restaurant. Wouldn't you have to wonder if these gigantic Twin Arrows marked this place in history of a "showdown" war between the Apache Indians led by Geronimo and the U.S. Army? It was pretty interesting. It made me want to stop inside the restaurant to interview a key historian, so I did.

Pulling up to the side of a windowed wall and leaning my bike against it was my only safe option for both security and physics, because of no bike locks or kickstand. As I entered through the door, bells were ringing, and a very pretty girl with very long black hair who looked like a waitress approached me for service. She said, "You look like you've come a long way from home."

I replied, "Yes! A very long way, over 1000 miles from Tulsa, Oklahoma, and I'm trying to make it to San Diego, California."

Then the waitress said, "Sit anywhere you would like. My name is Desiree if you need anything."

I responded, "Thank you. I had my last Hostess Twinkie and apple an hour ago, but I'm still hungry, so I think I'll order a hamburger."

The waitress took my order and said, "Okay, I'll put in your order right away."

So I sat at the bench table closest to the windows, in the "L" shape dining area to keep an eye on my bike, while she scurried over to put my order in. With this being a late lunch and not having a lot of customers at the moment, Desiree came back over to me, probably out of curiosity to probe me for a few questions.

She asked, "So why are you riding a bicycle so far? No one has ever come through here on a bike."

I answered, "I wanted a life-changing adventure to explore and at the same time I have a quest to make it to California to join the Marine Corps."

She also asked, "Aren't you afraid that it's pretty risky out on the road by yourself?"

I replied, "Well, I decided that this trip was the best thing for me to do, and there seemed to be no other choices in life. I have to see if I can reach San Diego, which means that I will have completed the journey and will have experienced a complete change of life. What it's been like to me is diving off the edge of a high cliff—it's impossible to ever return to the edge of that cliff as you're descending, and you hope to have a completely successful dive by surviving the entrance into the water below. You see, the high mountain cliff represents home, the long dive through the air is associated with the long drive on my bike, and then the landing in the water will be reaching my destination. Hopefully, my fate will not be to hit rock bottom, but to come back up to the top of the water alive and survive. Then it's a complete dive or complete change in life. One cannot do it without getting wet, and I cannot do this without taking the risk. What about you? Did you grow up here?"

Desiree said, "No, my home town is Kayenta. Mom needed to move here to cook and run the restaurant. But many years ago, my forefathers came from the Northern territories after many long hard winters, needing to hunt buffalo and be able to live off the land easier. My grandma stated that moving to Arizona was the best thing that happened to us."

I had to ask, "I'm sure you get a lot of comments about the giant twin arrows. Do they stand for any wars in the past?"

She said, "Mom and Dad tell me they are there for a memorial to the Indians, for fighting for peace to have our lands, and show as landmarks for travelers to stop. I'll go to check on your order and see if it's ready."

So now I'd found out what they believed the past history of the Twin Arrows was about. Lots of people had to wonder about this when they drove past. Back in Oklahoma, we didn't learn about it in the history books either, so I guess you had to walk, bike or drive here to discover for yourself.

As Desiree was ordering up the burger and fries, my eyes went on a scenic tour of all of the Western Indian memorabilia and many souvenirs hanging on the walls and in glass display cases.

Here she came. I told her, "You're sure covering a lot of bases, greeting, seating, waiting and serving." As she placed the plates before me, I asked her, "Are you planning to do any traveling?"

She responded, "Well, if I meet the right man and he wants to go places, I guess I'll leave Mom and Dad."

I felt like flirting, so I told her that she was so pretty, she could go to Hollywood in California and be a movie star. Her answer floored me, with what she said.

"Ah! A lot of that acting and pretending to be in love is taking up a person's life, while in real life I believe there's someone just for me and I need to hold out for true love."

Sounded good to me. Then other customers were coming through the door. With duty calling her to seat them, I began devouring my burger. With just the way Desiree had answered my questions and looking into those big brown eyes of hers, I discovered an attraction toward her, which sparked a fantasy of romance of sweeping her off her feet and taking her to California, convincing her that I'm the "someone just for her." Giving up on joining the Marine Corps for a special girl seemed a lot more fun and easier to do. Ah, kissy kiss, huggy hug, and fall madly in love. Bam!

I had to snap out my daydream, wearing the biggest smile, when Desiree side swiped me, saying, "Would you like a refill on your Coke?"

Then I smiled really big again, connecting with her sweet lips, and wanted to say, "Oh yeah, fill me up and kiss me all over," but instead gave her a quick Yes. How could I kid myself so much to think I could love her into frenzy and steal her away from her mom to take her on my bike? I was sure she would love riding on my handlebars or on top of my sleeping bag. Although, at night, it would be extra warm and cozy in my sleeping bag together. There I went fantasizing about her again.

Eating the last couple of bites of the burger slowly allowed me to savor the good flavor as my eyes were feasting on Desiree with the sweetest pictures to remember her by. How did you know, if you were to step out on a whim, like taking a chance to ask her to marry you, and she accepted, making you the happiest man for the rest of your life, or turned you down, causing disappointment for the rest of your life? Which would happen?

She noticed me looking at her moves and winked at me, doing a little flirting herself. I think she liked me too. With my romantic imagination going wild, all she would have to do was blow me a kiss, and I would have fallen right out of my seat, ready to say, "I love you."

Well, I had to pry myself away from my fantasies and take care of business. I spoke up saying, "Desiree! I'm ready for my check!" She acknowledged and brought it over to me. I left a tip as I whispered, "Maybe I'll come back for you some day." She smiled with a little twinkle in her eye. That was as good as a kiss of "I hope you do."

I got my coat, gloves, and cap together to mount my trusty steed. With lingering thoughts of Desiree, I pulled away onto the road again, fulfilling the slogan of, "Go West, young man, go West!"

CHAPTER 7

NEAR DEATH EXPERIENCE

My "Energy Tank" was full now, but my "Time Tank" was low. With the sun looking to have less than two hours left, I knew that I must make it to Flagstaff no matter what. I pumped the pedals up to full speed in tenth gear, thinking I could make the distance from where I was at now to the first motel I could find on the outskirts of town. I estimated about 20 to 25 miles. The analogy was if I kept up the speed of 20 mph, or rode each mile in five minutes, then I should get there before dark. But I would not know if I'd be slowing because of wind, ice, and snow, uphill climbing or fatigue. The scenic views were turning into more of a wilderness with evergreen shrubs and trees. It was a brand new environmental discovery for me. The headwind was starting to pick up, however, making it harder to keep up the pace above 20 mph and still admire the increasingly elevated hilly sightseeing. I was struggling to hold the bike straight on the outside line with sections of ice and snow on the edges of the roadway. My aim was intensifying, as I glanced at the map showing Flagstaff placed in my transparent protector on top of my handlebar bag. The map gave me an impression of maybe seven more miles, as I watched the last traces of the sunbeams start to go behind a thick overcast cloudy sky in the horizon, which meant it would actually get dark faster on this day. My assessment was that I must push harder, because without lights of any kind, how would I have any ability to hold the bike on the road, unless I had "night vision," until I saw a motel. I decided to be determined!

Now I was experiencing for the first time in my journey, the lonely-looking emptiness in this wilderness that was actually scary to me. I was actually sensing within my spirit a terrifying sensation, so much so that I couldn't force myself to sleep by the roadside, even if the darkness caught me. I was estimating at this point, about three miles to get there, but in a matter of minutes, the faint traces of the setting sun had quickly vanished beyond the mountains, leaving me pedaling the bike on the road in literal darkness. I started to panic as I squinted to try to see any kind of white line along the shoulder of the road between patches of ice and snow. Somehow I was trying to force my eyes to turn nocturnal—to see at night.

I came to a very high ridge of a huge mountain, seeing nothing, but anticipating the most gigantic downhill of Interstate 40 highway that I would ever come across in my life. This could be my last-ditch effort to get my speed up and climb the other side to reach a motel. It was the do or die finish line I must make. The strangest feelings were welling-up inside me, the panic and fear of the darkness in the wilderness were making it impossible to stop, which was also causing me to run on the pedals as fast as I could. With no other cars on the road at this time, I was a Lone Ranger streaking through the night. So much speed was being generated from my downhill momentum in tenth gear, I couldn't stop now! I felt like I was going 40 to 50 mph. Somehow, intuitively, I sensed that I could shoot across the bridge at the bottom, and the momentum would carry me up the steep mountain on the other side. Suddenly, a semi truck came speeding right behind me, entering the bridge at the same time I was. I looked back into his headlights, blinding me right at that moment, before I could get my head turned around. I couldn't see what was in front of me, and then BANG! I hit a huge ice-covered rock that instantly flipped me over in front of the semi truck. I fell down onto the bridge with the semi truck right on me. I thought he was running over me, but BING! I sprang up instanteously.

Right then and there, I should have been killed. In a split second of time, somehow, I came back up. I don't know how to explain it. Going against the laws of gravity and the force of a fall, I was literally brought back up from being knocked down. The very next split second, I felt the semi truck's earthshaking rumble and hurricane wind blowing past me, within inches of my head. Somehow, I was alive! It was a miracle! I didn't even believe in miracles or know that anything could happen supernaturally, but I knew it had just happened to me.

This had happened so fast, my head was spinning and I made to the other end of the bridge in a state of shock. The semi truck driver didn't stop and then disappeared over the top of the mountain ahead, just as fast as he came in behind me. I knew he had to be speeding excessively.

In reality, the laws of physics would explain, heavy objects fell due to force or gravity, and then it must take a greater force than the object's to reverse the fall. My fate "in the natural world" should have ended up being discovered the next morning in the newspaper headlines: LONE BIKER IS STRUCK DOWN BY SEMI TRUCK AND LEFT FOR DEAD. The driver probably didn't even see me in the dark, as I had no lights, and if he did see me go down and come back up, he probably couldn't believe his own eyes. The saying that it happened "faster than the eye could see," could this be the case? If there is a God in Heaven, could He take natural bad happenings and change them into a supernatural good that only He could do, to show us He is real? Then in this case, it is truth and the only way to explain this phenomenon.

I shifted down to seventh gear, encountering the base and middle incline of one of the largest mountain climbs yet—in the dark with only mere cloud glow. To keep my wits about me, my thoughts were overwhelmingly of what had just happened to me, knowing that I survived to forge ahead for the prize of a shower in a motel, and to have warmth and restoration for my exhausted body. Coming over the top of the mountain, pedaling a few more miles, in the distance I saw amber lights. Then, getting closer, my heart was starting to have joyful glee, making out a big red sign with big white letters saying, "Motel." Yeah! It had become reality; I was rolling into the driveway as if I were going across the finish line of a great race. I was huffing and puffing from both from the tough uphill climb, along with the dramatic panic from the near-death experience.

I leaned my bike alongside the motel office wall next to the door to see the clerk. I didn't see anyone at first, then a man came around the corner and said, "Do you want a room?"

I answered, "Oh yeah! Sure do! If only you could believe what I just went through to get here. I just about got ran over by a semi truck. I don't have any lights, and I hit a big rock that caused me to flip over in front of the speeding semi truck. Then something sprang me back up in a split second. I can't explain it, unless if God is real, He could have brought me back up."

The clerk said, "Wow! It sounds like you could have had a miraculous experience!"

Then I couldn't disagree and exclaimed, "I'm still in shock. I'm sure glad to be alive!"

So Mr. Clerk stated, "OK, Mr. Gabriel, how about I let you get you a nice hot shower in room five?"

I responded, "So you knew I was counting on taking a shower?"

He said, "Yep! I figured you've been through a lot and going a long way. Maybe you should take a car next time. It's a lot faster and a lot safer, you know!"

I replied, "Well, it's not the same, because I wanted it to be a challenge to see if I can make it to California."

He saw the determination in my face and conceded with his final comment: "I see your point—to find out if it will make you or break you and hope you'll survive your trip. Well, good luck!"

Then after collecting up my room receipt and key, I stepped outside to roll my battered and bruised 10-speed through the parking lot to room five. Without even parking the bike, I let it lean against me, as I tried the key and quickly rolled it inside the room. I was elated with both relief and joy to come to a little home of safety and warmth, making me feel as good as a king coming into his castle after a long hard journey.

I leaned the bike on a clear section of wall available, and then I immediately flung my body onto the bed, bouncing like a fat man on a trampoline and thinking, "Ah! I made it!" This was part of the victory spoils for crossing the finish line and surviving—just to have a soft, warm bed to lie upon. And! Just not that, but I had my very own TV for the night. WOW! I was in hog heaven. Quick, I had got to click it on to see if it worked? Oh yeah! It looked like a murder mystery to capture my suspense. Well! Suspense or not, I knew I had to tear myself away from the TV and jump into the shower.

So I stripped down, feeling like I was shedding a thick layer of skin, since I'd had these clothes on for so long. As I walked across the mirror buck naked, I shocked myself, seeing that I was so skinny from all of the pedaling and lack of Mom's good home cooking.

I darted through the shower curtains, grabbing the hot water faucet with impatience and eagerness. Cold water splashed me silly. Oh!!! Get me out of here! My rewarding hot shower instantly mortified and shocked me into a bit of anger, causing me to wonder if I was going to have to bear the cold to scrub off six days of stink. Dripping cold water, I called the motel office ,exclaiming, "I'm freezing with cold water." "What's going on?" the manager quickly said, "Oh yeah! The plumber forgot to turn the circuit breaker back on after replacing a broken pipe. Sorry about that, I'll get it turned on right away for you."

So now I was thinking how long before it would warm up? I guess it was better to wait rather than go to another motel room, since I'd just got a towel on, and I could get back into the murder mystery on TV.

I dozed off. Then all of a sudden, there were gunshots waking me up. Oh my gosh! I was shot! But, I wasn't bleeding or dreaming, it was coming from the TV, silly me. Well, I guessed the hot water was probably warmed up enough to try and take a shower.

I gingerly stretched my hand across the shower wall to turn-on the hot water knob and quickly recoiled from the ice cold water, so it would have time to heat up. Never did I think I would have to take what I had heard called a "Sailor's Shower," where you jumped in the cold water to just get wet, turned the water off, soaped yourself down, and then turned the water back on to rinse off. After a not-so-warm shower, I got more warmth from the towel, and I was so glad to be clean finally.

Funny thing was, I never had any pajamas for the whole trip—my riding clothes were my PJs, or you could say I was the man that rode the entire 1500-mile bike trip wearing pajamas.

Oh well, I wasn't about to put my riding gear back on with the road smell and all, so the next best thing was to feel those fresh clean sheets on my body and just sleep in the raw. Ah! Feels so good! Just in bed and watching TV, was giving me the rich man's feelings of "I got it made." Then road exhaustion and the traumatic brush with death had drawn me into sleepiness, so off I went into the night dreams.

My night seemed so short and went by in a snap! My eyes sprang wide open to see a ceiling of sheetrock instead of a ceiling of clouds or the sky, as I usually started all my days being outside. Knowing that I paid good money for this motel room caused me to enjoy lingering in bed longer than I should. But the cost of the room was not important enough compared to the cost of lost time and not arriving in California at the Marine Corps Depot by the deadline. So I sprang out of bed like I had pressed an eject botton and enjoyed another shower to wake up by. I quickly pulled on my riding clothes and thought about the luxury of being lazy to enjoy sleeping in, there in bed and just watching television all morning. But those temptations were counterproductive and I had to get motivated.

Well, I got all packed up and ready to roll the bike over to check out. I went to the manager's office, and he said, "I remembered you in room #5. With all that you've been through yesterday, I was really hoping the hot water would warm up for you. Did you get your hot shower taken?"

I replied, "Well, it later warmed up just enough."

He added, "I bet you feel a lot better and smell better."

I said, "Oh yeah!"

The manager gave me a good send off by saying, "Good luck! I hope you make it okay."

Upon that note, I shoved off from the manager's office, confirming in my mind that I did survive last night's near-death experience and that I did accomplish this goal to the Flagstaff Motel.

CHAPTER 8

WILDERNESS
SURPRISE ATTACK

I rolled down the motel driveway, back onto Interstate 40 and Route 66 at a lightning quick pace in eagerness to overcome any lost time and set out for my new short-term goal of climbing to the top of the Williams Mountains at 9,256 ft. elevation. After reaching the outskirts of Flagstaff, I was feeling good with renewed power, and my stomach growled with the energy of that of a tiger within, which passing an Exxon Gas billboard came to mind, saying, PUT A TIGER IN YOUR TANK. As I gained momentum, I was happy to take in the fresh scent of the pine trees and beautiful scenery that postponed the thoughts of eating food.

I covered many miles, encountering the highway curving in and around colossal towering cedar and pine trees. The "Tiger in my Tank" had run out of gas, since I had not eaten at all this day. So I pulled off the road and pushed my bike deep into a secluded area surrounded by the thick population of mountainous trees to look for small limbs, twigs, and leaves to pile together with rocks around them for a fire. After I lit my campfire inside the rocks, it started burning well enough to cook my oatmeal and sausage. Other than the smoke blowing in my eyes, the aroma was so enticing to my senses that I was ready for the sizzling sausage links to just jump right into my mouth. I quickly caught them between my teeth, and with a couple of chews, they went down faster than a shop vacuum sucking them in. I was elated at the moment to have a campsite setting, enjoying a "Carolina in the Pines" euphoria of this being a wonderful discovery.

Suddenly, things went blank. Several hours passed by unknowingly. The next thing that happened was I woke up flat on my back with this shrieking pain in back of my head and seeing the sun shining brightly through the tops of the trees. I was disillusioned in amnesia, not knowing where I was, how I got there, or why I was there. I don't know if someone tried to knock me out to rob me? I was out like someone turned off a light switch in my brain.

Now I was prompted by the need to escape the feeling of lostness and to find my way out of the wilderness and back to safety. So I gathered my things that were spread out all over, and it occurred to me that this could be evidence of someone rummaging through, looking for valuables. Suddenly, I started feeling afraid that someone was out there hiding behind the trees, watching me, that could have whacked me in the back of my head from behind and left me for dead. My hands were not working fast enough to pack up and avoid another surprise attack. As soon as I strapped my sleeping bag back on, I grasped the handlebars and started running alongside my bike as fast as I could to get out of the woods, hoping to find the road. I think it was an instinctive leading that kicked in to follow the more open area's flowing on a downward slope, which led me back to the highway. Whooo! I made it! I felt like I had escaped death back there in the woods.

I quickly mounted and pedaled as fast as I could, with my mind still in fear mode. I wasn't seeing any cars coming, which made me hog the road for more of an advantage to prevent unseen ice or obstacles knocking me off the bike.

After the blackout experience, my senses started coming back again. I felt like I had been dropped from the sky into another world of thick pine trees surrounding me and lining the sides of the highway. It was crazy, but maybe I should have been wearing a Superman cape by now, defying death, back to back, in two days. I thought, "Look out, world! Go ahead and come after me now, you can't keep me down! Naw!" That thinking was just too crazy. I didn't want to bring on another challenge of fate. That was like making a death wish.

Well, as I glanced down at my handlebar bag, I picked up my map showing my planned route going west through Arizona, which also was helping me to recover from my brief case of amnesia, as I became fixated on the renewed goal of reaching California.

"Shazam," I was back in the saddle again and back to my old self. Confidence returned to my soul's pursuit, was giving me determination that the energy is felt in my legs.

With lost time in the woods from being knocked out, I knew I had less time in this day now, so I was hoping to make it to the little town of Ash Fork.

I pumped out some fast miles and came rolling into more of the foothills terrain environment, with shorter cypress and cedar trees, just before sunset. I discovered a building beside the road with an old 1960 Chrysler Desoto car hanging off the rooftop. I figured that out because the big letters said, "Desoto's Salon, Route 66." It used to be a Texaco station in the 1950s. Now it was a barber and beauty shop with a gift shop for tourists. It was quite unique and one of a kind in the whole world.

That was enough history for now! After being knocked out, pedaling like crazy to escape, I think I was tired enough to roll out the sleeping bag to conclude this day's experience that I never wanted to repeat in my lifetime. Dreams are rare, but waking up finding yourself in a strange place from traveling every day, settling in after sunset, then waking up in different lighting because of the morning light, almost made it seem like you were opening your eyes into a different dream each time. It also had a surprising effect on me that caused me to spring into action.

I needed to launch out from Ash Fork and Desoto's Salon and look to Kingman, Arizona, which was over 85 miles away. This section of highway would probably be pretty desolate going through the Juniper Mountains and uninhabited country.

The sun increased its warmth as it arose, making me aware of the pace of time that I was needing to race against. The yellow hues of the early morning eastern sunrise changed midday into a brightness bringing out the greens of the trees and clear blue skies.

This long stretch of highway was zapping my water bottle supply with no towns in sight. To pedal faster, making up lost time without enough water, was leaving my throat parched and dehydrating my body. Now, this was the first time in my life to run out of resources, with no light at the end of the tunnel. I was exhausting all my liquids and foods that gave me energy. There were no towns on the map between here and Kingman. What was I going to do? I didn't know! I had better hope if I was lying alongside of the road, dying of thirst, that somebody would stop and pour water down my throat to revive me. But right now, I was taking the last two gulps from my water bottle to relieve the parchedness. I felt like the lone survivor in a movie, determined to "Make it to California or Bust," and it was going to take every ounce of fortitude in this body to push myself to make it there, to live or die trying.

I came into a very shaded, curvy section of highway, looking up seeing a running mountain stream. I took my water bottle and collected up some "Rocky Mountain High" waters to allow me to live a little longer, hopefully long enough to discover an unknown supply. Now, I would surge forward, trying to over-come the mental challenge of needing fluids and making it to Kingman, which was becoming more impossible with the very extreme distance. But all that my mind, soul and body knew to do was to keep pushing. There was no glory for quitters or giv-ing up. Especially, on what was a monumental life goal and to remember that everything is hinged on this and a pivotal motivation for the rest of my life. Then I had an epiphany: I'm caught up in the moment of my life's purpose in adventure, in all my 18 years, coming to "find a man in the wilderness." Hopefully, this man would come out of the wilderness.

I believe I came into an experience of a rare happening of life which physically, how could I possibly make it, but an internal fortitude transcended time, and I found myself rolling into Hot Rod Café along Route 66, Kingman, Arizona. What a relief! The instant I grabbed a waitress, named Niki, I ordered a glass of water, and I felt like that was a life-saving checkpoint. They had what looked close to a 1938 Ford classic racer in front.

She knew from seeing me riding up on a 10-speed bicycle, looking like a desert traveler, worn down from dehydration and physical exhaustion, that this was crucial drinking water for me. I drank down the water so fast; it went down in just a couple of gulps. After about the third refill, I started breathing normal again and ordered a chicken club sandwich with, of course, a fourth refill. My plight for the only objective possible—to reach out harder than ever before—had come true. I survived to this point, but I was feeling like a beggar in the "City Palace" of Kingman, Arizona. I wolfed down the chicken club sandwich and gulped down the life-sustaining water. The waitress was probably thinking I was on my last leg and she had never seen someone so desperate for drinking that much water.

Then Niki asked, "How long has it been since you've had water out there on the road?"

I replied, "About fifty miles back for almost the whole day, except for a little stream water. But this was the hardest experience for the third time, not knowing if I would live or die." I could tell looking into Niki's eyes, she was being sympathetic and had turned to showing an interest in what I'd been through. I told her about being lucky to be alive from how I was just about ran over by a semi truck two nights ago, knocked down in front of the truck and somehow sprang back up. Then two mornings ago, I had a surprise attack, being knocked out while eating a breakfast in the woods near Flagstaff.

Niki was mesmerized. She said, "I just can't imagine how anyone could go through so much in such short time."

The manager, overhearing our conversation, came over to tell me, "Young man! That's one of the most dramatic life experiences I've ever heard. Don't worry about the sandwich and chips, they're on the house."

I responded, "Oh! Thank you, sir."

"You're welcome," he said.

As I looked the part of a homeless traveler, he treated me with a real warm consideration.

This was also a breakthrough, using everything except a few dollars I had left hidden inside my handlebars. It was helpful people like him, who were willing to cover a meal, or those who allowed me to stay in their houses along the way, that were making this 1500-mile journey possible. This was an impossible trip to estimate costs, bring enough food, water, and provisions, or even know where I would end up staying from one night to the next night, because each mile traveled was a new discovery. For most of my stops, I was usually running out of daylight, and it was pitch dark. Then I was forced to the side of the road in the middle of nowhere land. With no lights, there was no choice but to roll out the sleeping bag and rough it out until sunrise. This would be the case tonight, because I just couldn't conveniently stop where I'd seen a shelter to sleep, then waste the daylight travel time available. So the quick split from the Hot Rod Café to get going to California was essential. How could a person even think of sleeping when standing next to a race car, with thoughts of how fast it would go? So with a good meal, lots of water and getting psyched up as if I was drag racing, there was no other faster 10-speed. It was firsthand nature for me to react like a fish in water when burning daylight. I had to push the pedal to the metal. I was heading to Yucca, Arizona.

Just as fast as my drinking water went down the tubes when I was dying of thirst back at the Hot Rod Café, so I saw the sun plunging rapidly as fast into the western horizon.

Another day in the bag, with a thankful heart that I made it back there to find provisions.

CHAPTER 9

A CHUCK AND SPARKIE CHRISTMAS

There was a loud rumble coming from the cloud formation with the rising sun, sounding like a possible early morning snowstorm brewing, that woke me up. I reacted instinctively to immediately pack up my bike to get on the road quickly. Hopefully I could try and outrun the threatening wintry blast. As I looked back, I could see lightning setting the clouds aglow. This reminded me of the one time I had ever seen the effects of snow storm clouds having lightning in them, when I was 11 years old, after the power was knocked out at night and the clouds lit up with orange, pink and bright blue. But that was from the safety of looking out of our front bay window. It was scary enough then, but now, the thunderous monster chasing me caused me to pedal frantically, like a bat out of hell, completely vulnerable to whatever fell from the sky. Having no protection and no shelter around, I was duped. I felt like I had a chance to make it to Yucca if I kept up my slightly downhill pace at close to 35 mph and beat the monster. With so many things happening to me in the last three days, like the near-death experiences, I started thinking maybe I needed to learn how to pray. It would be nice to know that Mom probably could be praying for me back home right about now. No way to know. Did that praying stuff really work? I just knew what I was seeing now, and it didn't look good. The skies were darkening around me with rain sprinkling for the next 4 miles. Then a bolt of lightning struck somewhere, changing the rain into snow. I guess I was caught! A sudden frigid blast of wind frosted my nose and eyebrows. This was no picnic! In fact, it was panic time. As the snow thickened, it become a white wall to fight through with the upcoming miles. The shoulder of the road became harder to stay on, and I had to slow my pace down. I was forced to have a death grip on the handlebars as the narrow tires didn't have much traction at this point and I was terrified that I would slide off the side of the road, not being able to see what the snow was hiding now. "Gosh! What am I to do if something breaks down?" I thought.

Lo and behold, the upcoming sign said, Yucca 7 miles. Yeah! I was figuring out that I could make it in about 45 minutes and then head for cover, as long as the bike held up. Being wet and woolly, had caused me to ride heavier and harder. But once again, it was mind over matter with determination that counted. By keeping my momentum up, I was risking it all by slipping and sliding along the way. If I stayed in one place for too long, needing help from this heavy snowstorm, I could have been covered in a white blanket and hidden from any rescuers. Got to keep shaking it off!

While I was striving to reach any signs of life and straining with my eyes to see through the thick snowflakes, a gas station sign finally became visible. When I saw an awning to get out of the snowstorm, I steered my snow-impacted bike to get under it, like a boat overtaken by giant waves in a storm that barely made it to shore. Weighted down with the threat of failure, I felt relieved as I compared myself with the analogy of a visual picture of a drowning man yelling for help and then managing to grab a floating tree trunk to save himself.

Even being under the awning, I was being chilled from the brisk wind. When I entered through the front doors, my snow-packed boots caused me to skate across the store's tiled floors. I asked the store clerk to borrow a broom to knock off the impacted snow from my bike.

He said, "What's your name?"

"I'm Daniel," I replied.

"Well, Daniel, I've never seen anyone in my life ride a bike in a snow storm. Where are you heading?" he inquired.

"California!" I exclaimed. "I've come all the way from Tulsa, Oklahoma."

He said, "Holy moly there, man! How do you do it in all of this snow?"

I answered with, "Well, I almost lost my life a couple of times. Then people were willing to help me out. I have been on a driving determination to reach San Diego to join the Marine Corps."

Then he was impressed with my accomplishing my insane trip thus far and he said, "Here's the broom, and when you come back in, I'll fix a hot chocolate for you."

"OK, that sounds great!" I exclaimed. So I jumped back outside and started brushing into the cold wind, which was helping making the snow go aloft. I imagined that if you could weigh the bike and gear before with the snow and ice, then after I brushed it off, it probably would weigh 20 pounds lighter. I swept off his entrance as a courtesy to him.

He said, "You're so deserving of this hot chocolate. Finish it and I'll get you another one."

I didn't refuse. When I finished, I said, "Thank you very much."

He said, "You're very welcome, and I wish you lots of luck to make it to San Diego."

Then with a few customers standing in amazement that they would never try what I'm doing, I pulled my cap and gloves on, mounted the bike, and started plowing through the snow.

"The store clerk and customers had become like a fan club cheering me on," I ventured to think. This was a positive perk to get me going again. As I was going a little farther south and west, it was still snowing but not as windy. I thought if I would persevere, I might just outrun the bad weather conditions and try to cross over the Arizona and California borderline, a monumental achievement.

Along Route 66, I discovered a little museum stop at Cool Springs, with ten different country flags flying above the Mobil Gas pump insignia, which was a winged flying horse. It appeared to be famous, with celebrities' pictures inside. All of these little souvenirs were so neat that it was hard to resist buying them.

I had to get myself back on the road again. Fortunately, the weather had calmed down with the sun breaking through the clouds. Coming past Topock, you would see three major signs, 1. For Lake Havasu recreation, 2. Colorado River. As you crossed over the bridge, 3. the biggest, most important sign: YOU ARE NOW ENTERING CALIFORNIA! Yippee! I could have shouted upon the mountaintops, I MADE IT! I was elated. My announcement and celebration was silent. However, in my heart of imagination, I was riding down the middle of a huge football stadium with all of the crowd cheering. This was what it was like: Seeing so many various hilly Mohave Desert terrain features, some snow-capped tops, some large exposed tree-sized cactus, the lake and river waters, made you want to stop and explore. My limited time didn't allow for excursions now. But the Grand Canyon, Lake Havasu and Zion Park would be at the top of my favorites to see. But for now, I wanted to continue this noteworthy, "Fireworks Experience" of riding on California highways.

Coming into Needles, California, on Christmas Eve, I was finding spotty patches of snow left over from the snowstorm that I was riding in most of the day. It was very quiet here, so cold, and the daylight was about to flee. There was a bird dog running wildly, barking at me, with an old man trying to call him back. "Sparkie! Get back here." I stopped to greet him. The old man came over to retrieve Sparkie.

"Hey, mister! Do you know of any place that I could stay the night?" I said to him.

He replied, "Maybe. Where are you from?"

"Tulsa, Oklahoma," I answered.

He was quite friendly as he introduced himself. "My name's Chuck. Wow, that's along way off."

"I'm Daniel. I'm trying to make it to San Diego."

"Where do you think I could stay?"

Chuck said, "Well, I'll tell you what, why don't you come on over to my place? It's real small, but it's warm, and you can get out of the cold and the snow."

I thought that sounded great. So I dismounted and walked my bike over to his place, which was an older dwelling. He allowed me to roll my bike into what was a very small, 12' x 30' room, that had a bed and two chairs in the living room serving as his bedroom too, and then a curtain pulled around the corner where the shower and toilet were. It was what you would call a shack.

Chuck spoke up and said, "I know this is not much, but I call it home."

"I'm so glad to meet you and Sparkie. Have you lived here for very long?"

Chuck said, "Naw, it's been eight years since I lost my wife, lost my job, lost my house and lost my friends. Now all I have is old Sparkie."

"How did all of that happen?" I replied. I was shocked that he had gone through so much tragedy.

Then Chuck began to spill it out. "We had a real nice house just outside of Las Vegas and a well-paying job. I started gambling a lot because it was a lot of fun, made some friends by giving them money to play games and drink together. It grew into such an overwhelming addiction that I spent more on all of that than I could ever pay back, so my wife found out, and we were forced into bankruptcy. The bank took the house from us, and the wife divorced me. All I had left was a car and my dog to drive here to Needles. As soon as I got here my uncle offered to help me out and pay for this low-rent place because I had no where else to live."

I said, "Wow! I've never known that so much trouble can happen to one person. So what do you do for money now?" "I'm a stocker at the Safeway grocery store on Main Street," he answered and then said, "Hey! Why don't we have us a little dinner? I'll see what I've got. Would you believe it? On Christmas Eve, I'm out of soup, canned food, and stuff to make a dinner? But I have chips, orange juice, and I can make us some peanut butter and jelly sandwiches. What do you think?"

I told him, "That's okay with me."

So I shed the cold wet clothes, showered and pulled on a borrowed bathrobe, which felt so good while my clothes dried. I sat down with Chuck and Sparkie to enjoy a peanut butter and jelly sandwich in the warmth of their home. This was one of the most different and humbling Christmas Eves that I ever will have in my life to remember.

Chuck had one of the smallest televisions I ever did see. The screen was no bigger than a cantaloupe, and it picked up three fuzzy channels. It was nice to have somewhat of a small family atmosphere dinner and a Christmas show on to enjoy for a change.

After we chomped down our last bites of sandwiches, Chuck put on a little show with Sparkie, doing tricks of roll over, fetch, jump up for a catch, and a backward somersault off the door. I applauded, and Sparkie got extra treats for his great performance.

In comparison to my journey's unpredictable forced stops in the night which could be anywhere alongside an unknown road, this was an experience like a stranger giving to a beggar. I felt privileged to have someone not very well off himself invite me in and show kindness toward me at just the right time.

Chuck offered me half his bed with a curtain rod down the middle. I said, "Thanks, but I can make do with my sleeping bag on your floor, which, coming from mostly hard dirt and rocks to lay on, will be more than comfy enough for me."

Chuck warned me by saying, "If that's what you want to do, I can't protect you against scorpions or spiders down there, but Sparkie may just warm up to you, and maybe he'll protect you."

Then I thought that could be a likeable situation, so I told Chuck, "Okay, I'll let Sparkie sleep with me."

So I stretched out the sleeping bag in between the foot of the bed and the wall. Sure enough, after turning all the lights out, Sparkie came over to pull on the corner of my sleeping bag to share with him. He got to kind of growling, suggesting we play tug of war. "Come on, Sparkie! Let's go to sleep, boy," I said. After some snarls, he conceded and lay down alongside me. During the night sometime, I woke up, hearing Sparkie have muffled barks and kicking out his legs, like he was chasing rabbits in his dreams or sensing scorpions getting close, but still asleep the whole time. What a night!

When I woke up, Chuck was frying up some eggs and bacon. He saw that I was stirring about and said, "MERRY CHRISTMAS! Come on Daniel and Get up, I've got some breakfast for you."

I replied, "It is Christmas. Oh, that's so nice of you to fix that." I could tell that Chuck was enjoying my company this whole time. I hoped that he would reach out and make more friends in the future. He held himself back, living in a hermit lifestyle, probably because of getting hurt so bad in the past.

We sat down to enjoy his good hot breakfast, and Chuck asked me, "What are you going to do if you make it to San Diego? That is still a long way to go by bicycle."

"Yep! I figure that I've ridden about 1,175 miles, and I have about 325 miles to go. I've got just 7 days to make it by January 1, because when I get there, I'm going through the Marine Corps gates to boot camp."

Then Chuck said, "Well, boy, you're cutting it pretty close."

I responded, "I've come this far. I could have gotten killed a couple of times back there on the road. Having come through so much at this point, I'm bound and determined with all I've got to make it."

Chuck was quite impressed with all of this. Maybe with him seeing me doing something daring, he just might be encouraged to do more with his life.

I rolled up the sleeping bag, packed up my stuff, and prepared to shove off. Chuck gave me another sandwich and an apple for the road and said, "I'm glad we met. You'll probably be the only person on the road with a bicycle today, since it is Christmas."

I told him, "Probably so. Thanks for the meals and taking me in out of the cold."

The last thing Chuck said was, "I wish you good luck. I hope you make it to San Diego. Call me if you need any help."

What a great send off! I felt charged up with his backing to feel so motivated! My pedaling started off so effortlessly with new views of more Christmas decorations and seeing lights still turned on at various houses, showing their colorful merry spirits. I knew I would be counting down the miles and days now.

CHAPTER 10

WATER SKIING AND CAMPING

There was still a patchy coverage of snow, which qualified for a white Christmas after all! If you were to see this terrain from a helicopter, it would show so many mixtures of green, brown and tan hills with a whipped cream topping. I had a long stretch of road, which revealed more of the shoulders and hardly any traffic. I guessed everyone was at home, having family over or just staying inside for Christmas. It made it lonely out there, causing me to remember the Charles Bronson song again, with a line saying, "Going down that long lonesome highway." With no one around, having the whole road to myself, I felt like popping a wheelie, but that would put a lot of strain on the rear wheel with all the luggage weight being carried and could break more spokes again. I had to control my "Wild March Hare" urges and keep both wheels down on the road.

I encountered a wild December head wind, though, that shook me back and forth like salt and pepper shakers, juggling my balance a lot. This made for a long day going to Essex.

Needing to utilize as much wheel time as possible, I had daylight to keep going through town and planned to stop only when it was absolutely dark. After staying inside on a nice, cozy, warm floor last night, I thought that tonight it would probably be a freezing cold dirt bed on the shoulder of the road, throwing myself back in the survival mode again.

One of my main concerns for the entire trip, so far, had been the tires holding pressure, which always caused me to look down at the point of contact "where the rubber meets the road" to see if they looked flat. I had added air from my frame pump occasionally, which had been a lifesaver. Without it, I would have been walking many miles and would definitely not have made it on time to the Marine Corps Depot by January 1st. With increased inflation, actually found it easier to pedal. Unfortunatly, the tires could have slid a lot in the ice and snow, causing me to lose control more and off the road more. So it was a fine line. I could have lowered the pressure, creating more traction, but I couldn't go too low or I'd risk ruining the tube by pulling the valve stem and causing a leak. Right now I was pumped up and had the front wheel pointed toward Ludlow about 35 miles away. It was going to be a "bright, bright sunshiny day" with the sky looking so clear.

One thing about being on this journey that I came to realize was that I had discovered a new freedom being aloft most all the time. The other side of the coin of this journey ironically, required me to stay within the boundary of the highway, as it told me where to go and what to do, making me stay within the lines, allowing no excursions. So discipline and determination went hand in hand. The sun warming my back seemed to propel my speed even more, knowing that if I made the most of it, I'd be rewarded by gaining more miles to beat the clock.

I wondered if anyone ever came from the big cities to go to the small towns. In all of the small towns I rode through, some people had never heard the names of these small towns or heard where they are located. But the advantage I had was actually getting a taste of what those small towns were like, by riding slow enough to tour them and converse with some of the local population. This is a great way to encounter, the climate, culture, history and different types of people.

Strangely enough, the railroad came the closest to Route 66 right after Needles, California, since there were are no other stops or life support for hundreds of miles in any direction. It was probably because of the emptiness of the Mojave Desert that I was going through.

Coming up on Ludlow, California, the town looked very small. It had one gas station, café and motel. I stopped for food and water, because the map had shown a long line without any dots for other towns going through the desert. Coasted alongside the diner's windows, and then I leaned my weathered loaded, down bike next to the door. After walking through the doors, I encountered a very short, round, chunky waitress, eager to greet me and say, "You're probably ready for a big steak and baked potato."

Then I said, "Do I look that hungry?"

"Yes, you do, riding a bike like you're doing. I can tell from all your bags that you're not just out for a Sunday ride," she said. I could tell that she had not missed a meal in a long time and she probably did a lot of taste-testing." Nevertheless, she took good care of me, filled my water bottles, and gave me some chocolate chip cookies for the road ahead. She was a real aggressive young lady, wanting to talk me into staying at the motel where she stayed, which had a game room, lounge and lots of pictures of history.

I kind of thought that she was pretty friendly and we would have had a lot to share. However, I had some more daylight to burn so I hit the road thinking that if I had been persuaded to accept her invitation, what could have happened? I felt like I would have lost out on my game plan, being so close to completion.

People's pursuit of happiness in their journey may be compared to a flock of geese migrating south for the winter. They fly by an instinctive directive route programmed in their brains. They came from somewhere up north, straight as the crow flies to the southern regions. You don't usually hear of a whole flock of geese taking an excursion over to Hawaii to stroll along the beaches for a couple of weeks and then go south. Even though it's nice and toasty there. So I was also being instinctive like the geese, but instead of going south, I wanted to "go west young man, go west." I'd stick to the route in order to hopefully achieve my goal.

Since I resisted the temptation of the fun and games with the waitress, I was back on course and energized to hit tenth gear, riding wide open. With this being the Mojave Desert, there were a lot of white sandy moguls with spotty, desert bushes and cactus spread around at random. Not much to survive on out here for snakes, rabbits, lizards, coyotes and other game. Occasionally, I saw box turtles trying to cross the road. I stopped and scooted them over to the other side because I couldn't bear to think about them getting run over.

I was reminded of catching turtles at the lakes in Oklahoma. Mom and Dad took my sister Sheila and me quite often to Ft. Gibson Lake or Keystone Lake to camp out. I remember setting up our tents after my dad pulled off a water skiing stunt with me on his shoulders. Mom drove the boat for the first time I'd ever seen her do it. When Sheila saw me on Dad's shoulders, she yelled for Momma to go faster. I think I was screaming loudest because when you're five years old and you're all of a sudden flung up that high, you're feeling like you're on a roller coaster out of control and wondering if you could fall to your death at any moment. Dad's traumatizing experience convinced me early in life that running off and joining the high-flying circus act was not for me.

That evening, Mom fired up the Coleman stove to cook up beef stew and potatoes. I went out with my sister to hunt for critters. The most intriguing creatures to me were the crawdads and snapping turtles. Sheila hated the crawdads because I grabbed them behind the pinchers and became a monster, chasing her while holding them, causing her to scream all the way back to camp. Dad scolded me and ordered me to throw the crawdads back in the lake. I found two turtles, and Dad let me take them home, but not the crawdads. Shucks! Could have had a lot of fun with my sister.

That night, a storm rolled in with everyone sleeping soundly. I woke up hearing the heaviest rain that I'd ever heard before. It was pouring down, with the wind blowing fiercely and thunder so loud it was shaking the ground. Then EL ZAPPO, a crack of lightning struck right beside the tent. I felt stunned, causing me to jump up and yell, "Dad, we've been hit by lightning." I was ready to run for my life. Dad told me to lie back down, stating that we couldn't go anywhere due to the pouring rain out there and just to go back to sleep. I thought, "What? How can I sleep in this thundering and lightning?" It's a scary feeling like you're going to be zapped and fried alive or washed away by the flooding rain. We didn't get much sleep that night. But I got to take two box turtles home with me.

Since turtles liked the dirt a lot, I dug out this great big "fox hole" with rocks, plants, and a little pond at the bottom. I collected more turtles, beetles, and bugs to make an impressive exhibit for all my friends. Mom and Dad seemed to trust me with all of the excavations of the dirt home for the turtles and keeping myself from the hazards of the turtles snapping off all of my fingers. I guess they had observed that I had fast enough reactions and how I could handle them with caution. In my perception of how I was viewed by my pet turtles, I was their big friend, even though in actuality, I captured them and I was holding them as little slaves that I could maybe have do tricks for me.

But I always provided a needed supply of food and water for the turtle colony, so maybe they really did respect me for that. After all, they shouldn't bite the hand that fed them, right?

I had been riding the rest of the afternoon with my head in the clouds, thinking about the best of the lake experiences, like Dad teaching me to water ski at nine years old. I fell a lot of times, drinking more lake water than I wanted, but I finally learned to keep my knees bent, hold my skis parallel in front of me, staying balanced, to get on top of the water. I was able to ski for quite some distance. Now that was a blast! Water skiing became my most favorite lake event far above any other, as I would encounter wave jumping, quick jet turns, and even a need for speed. Motorcycling and bicycling were the greatest influences in my life, since I could go wherever I wanted and at whatever time, seeing so many places in Oklahoma. I learned early when I was younger to do the mechanics on what I was riding, to make them work well and be reliable for the trips I took.

With the bike holding together for the time being, my mind was relieved from any worries to bring all of my daydreaming back to the reality of riding on Route 66. Hopefully, I was fulfilling my dream of finding a new life and successfully completing this 1500-mile trip to San Diego. Taking time to reminisce about the building of my model cars made the miles go faster. I had over a hundred cars displayed on my bedroom bookshelves like a big national car show. My favorites were the racing Mustangs and Corvettes. I had worked with so much paints and tubes of glue, it was a wonder I never got high on that stuff or my brain cells weren't toasted.

The preoccupation of such good memories made time pass quickly. I discovered that the sun was falling fast, trying to put a close to this day and causing darkness to cut me short of reaching Barstow by maybe 20 miles. So I was riding on such a completely barren and empty flat road offering nothing at all for a place to sleep. I literally had to roll the bike away far enough to hide from traffic, bandits, and to deaden the noise of the vehicles behind some desert bushes. I rolled out my sleeping bag and hoped there would not be any unexpected critters wanting to crawl inside with me tonight.

I awakened with the cold morning dew on my forehead. This was almost the same effect of my mom spraying a cold mist on my face to get me up for school in the morning at home. This was so uncomfortable though, that I packed as fast as I could, pulled on my boots and jumped on the road to dry out. I pulled out the rest of the chocolate chip cookies the waitress gave me a couple of days ago to munch on for breakfast. I was not going to let the cold dew put a damper on my day; instead, I treated myself to have a happy stomach.

As happened numerous times throughout the journey, the overcast cloudy skies prevented seeing the sun to give a reference to the time of day. I knew the need for "pedal to the metal" speed was most important to offset complacency because I knew that time would pass too fast to keep track of it.

As I rode west on Route 66, I watched the super long trains coming alongside the highway from the north and east funnel into Barstow, which gave me enthusiasm to be as fast as a speeding locomotive. I could not have planned this any better because of the quick time I needed to make and it seemed to be paying off.

Even scores of semi trucks along the highway heading in that direction. I looked on the map; Barstow was in the middle of Southern California, surrounded by the Mojave Desert, with other cities many miles away. As a matter of demographics, they probably made it Grand Central Station for all of the trains running through from all directions. There's even a McDonald's on Route 66 in which they took real train cars and used them for the restaurant and named that "Central Station." If you'd never been on a train before, here was the chance to have a hamburger and be on one, without paying the high price for a train ticket. I liked how they painted the train cars and different sections of the McDonald's building with different bright colors. Definitely eye catchers to all the motorists coming into town.

My westerly pursuit of finding my route to San Diego was taking a dramatic turn to the south after going through Barstow. My map guided me onto Highway 15 South to Victorville, which was more than 40 miles away, meaning that I most likely would not make it before the sunset, no matter how fast I drag raced to get there. But I could say that at this point, in an overwhelmingly long biking journey, I was coming down the home stretch to MCRD, the Marine Corps Recruit Depot in San Diego.

While making progress heading south, I saw the Sidewinder Mountains off to the left of my long-range telescoping view at 5,274 ft. elevation, which looked ghostly with the wintry gray from the cloud cast in the distance. Was this a sign of another subfreezing night for me to endure? With my expectation of going south, I hoped to have warmer conditions to discover. This section of highway, which was both Highway 15 and Route 66 synonymously, had a heavy load of traffic, some probably going home from visiting at Christmas time and coming from all of the northern parts of California.

There was nothing like being hit by a blast of wind draft from a passing semi truck on a 10-speed. It was almost earth -shattering and downright scary at the same time. Although the actual draft was a pulling effect, helping me to gain speed, after I realized that I was not actually physically being run over, I was ecstatic that my life was spared again and many times over.

CHAPTER 11

AIRPLANES AND DREAMS OF FLYING

The map shows the SCLA, which is the Southern California Logistics Airport, where this is a transitional landing strip for military, commercial and obsolete aircraft that, interestingly enough, go through hangers for testing, annualizing and classifying hundreds of planes each year. They can be decommissioned, repaired or parted out. So their fate is decided and they may be flown into the bone yard, which had become the graveyard for thousands of aircraft that had been in airline operations for many years. As I drew nearer to Victorville, roughly seven miles to the south, I saw quite a few military aircraft flying over to the landing strip. There were B-52 bombers, DC-10s, Boeing 747s, etc., at the SCLA airport.

Along with the planes landing in the western skies, so was the sun landing on the western horizon to turn out the lights for this day, stopping me in my tracks somewhere short of Victorville. Feeling the bite of the nippy winds prompted me to quickly dive into the sleeping bag tonight. Sheer darkness and exhaustion coupled with the cold caused me to cuddle up in a fetal position, relaxing me physically, which freed up my mind to energize my remembrance of my reoccurring dream of flying ever since I was six years old. After being in a deep sleep, I opened my eyes, looking up into the dark sky, having this exhilarating feeling of an upward thrust so thrilling that I was flying up into the night sky as if my bed had sprouted wings with rocket engines, taking me to outer space. Then lights in the distance caused my flying bed to be drawn to it. To witness this sight from a distance was like looking down from outer space, seeing a huge glowing spot on the planet. The closer I got, I saw changing colors from what appeared to be a giant Ferris wheel, then a rocket orbiter and many other rides with such bright illumination. This was a huge National Fair going on. I flew over the entire fair, close enough to hear the laughter, the screams, and the crowd cheering from whichever of the rides they were on. Then with the electrifying excitement of all the people beaming up to me, it triggered my airplane bed into upside down loops and corkscrew maneuvers as I moved my bedpost bars like a stunt pilot putting on an air show for all of the fair people. I was flying in figure-eight patterns, flipping upside down and back around again. Wow! Shouts of acclamation confirmed that they were having one of the happiest times in their lives, as I was somehow pulling off these amazing stunts. As I was flying so many corkscrews and loops, around and around, I was getting dizzy and started to black out. Then I woke up to the reality of it being just a dream.

I awoke early with the sound of the thundering semi trucks roaring down Highway 15 and jet planes overhead going in and out of the airport. Most of my journey had made me feel like a lone ranger on a very lonely, long, desolate route, trying to make it to my destination alive. But now, nearing Victorville, I saw the first signs of the big city and big state of California effects of heavy traffic and huge populations. I hit the road, encountering some wind turbulence, in which the weight of my baggage played a role in giving me more counterbalance to keep the wind and the semitruck drafts from pulling me in front of traffic that could easily run me over. I was finally seeing buildings on the outskirts of Victorville, and in the background I see the San Bernardino Mountain Range kind of in a blue haze. There were a lot of businesses strung together along the highway here. There was another Route 66 Museum, which had so much memorabilia, it would probably take over six hours to go through, covering more than 4,500 square feet of space.

For the record: Route 66 was a historical highway that started in November 11, 1926. It traverses about 2,600 miles from Chicago, Illinois, to Los Angeles, California, through eight states. Many thousands of people were looking for their fortunes and happiness taking this route of travel. Many were answering the call, "go west young man, go west." This indeed was called the "Mother Road" and the "Main Street of America." I was so glad to see and discover some retained facts of American history along my journey. It definitely added to the perspective of finding a new life that so much had happened before to get me here.

I was making history for my life now. I felt like I could not have gotten anywhere to learn about the outside world if I stayed in Tulsa. This trip had already changed my outlook on life with so many different experiences.

I conquered some mileage to reach new cities. According to the map, on the east side of Los Angeles there were numerous suburbs with foreign names like Ontario, China Hills, and Corona that I would be riding through. With the big town life and many cars on the highway, I felt overwhelmed, feeling small as an ant about to get crushed by everything being so much larger.

Drawing close to San Bernardino was a milestone marker of 1400 miles. It was just 100 miles away from San Diego, my final destination completing my journey's quest. I would have pedaled about 60% of Route 66, 2,600 miles of the Mother Road in the western United States. I don't know if I could say that my body was worn out with blisters, sore muscles, and aches, but the bike tires were almost worn bald, and the chain with the derailleur was squeaking badly, needing lubricant.

My first impressions of Southern California, which I was finding in the heavy traffic and businesses so far, was a fast-paced atmosphere compared to Tulsa, which was very laidback. I couldn't help but notice the many motorists speeding past me, looking back through the rear glass, making me feel like a crazy man or one of a kind, since I was riding a bike instead of driving a car. I guess I could be looked at as going against the grain of the old saying, "birds of a feather, flock together." Well, I felt like a "black bird on wheels," finding a different way to fly. Of course, I was an unusual traveler with a packed-down bike on the freeway. There hadn't been any other bicyclist seen here or in the whole 1400 miles that I rode on these cross-country highways and freeways. With 100 miles to go and two days before I'd pass through the Marine Corps gates, I was going to estimate that this would be my last two nights of sleeping as a civilian, and then I would turn into a soldier.

For now, I felt the effects of a long fast-paced ride among the Californian drivers, and it wore me out. I actually saw a roadside rest stop with picnic tables that made it good for an open sky bedroom to see the stars. These were the wooden types with a slight amount of flexibility that were more preferable than the cold concrete. Better than an old drafty motel with a pungent smell that you dreaded to breathe in. The moon was out, providing some background lighting. It was hard to have any privacy with cars and trucks pulling in and out, using the restrooms. I decided to pull the edge of the sleeping bag over my eyes and ears to try and block it out.

At some time in the night, I woke up to walk over to the restrooms. My drowsiness went directly into daylight and weightlessness. I felt a change in my awareness of a loss of gravity, and after a couple of steps I could supernaturally leap over obstacles, my body becoming as aloft as a bird. But I was doing this like I was born with this ability and could always fly whenever I wanted to and wherever I wanted to go. It was feeling so real and so natural, with no fear of falling, as I was going higher and higher. I actually went over treetops, seeing other birds flying at the same level, and then buildings, with other people waving out of the windows. I felt like I was invincible, becoming a new creature with no limits and having no wings or anything to assist me in flying. I had decided to really turn on the jets to see how fast my body really would go, maybe over 500 mph. Then I crashed into a high-rise building that popped up. I woke up, realizing it was just a dream. My long expedition on land was somehow being rewarded now in dreams with the ease and speed of flying to cover the country that I couldn't see by land.

I remembered from high school what Henry Wadsworth Longfellow had said: "The Man Without Dreams is Like a Bird Without Wings." I think I wanted to adopt this as my own life's philosophy and hear about other people living out their dreams.

A new day dawned, and now with a just few dollars left, an apple, crackers, and water in my bottle, I hoped I could stretch what little I had left to the end. There were a lot of cars, trucks, and activities along the road so early in the morning. Well, my expedition just got riskier because of a higher chance to get taken out by all of these crazy California drivers. I had heard that before from people, saying, "You've got to watch out for those wild and crazy people out there." Now I remembered Mom's advice, saying, "You better take your 1940 Chevy Coupe for the protection." That mode of transportation was not a memory I wanted to make and was still so far from being creative or taking the trip with any dignity. I really wanted to do this with style. Well, even if I didn't look in good style, being pretty road worn and weathered, I decided to grin and bear it. I had to figure out when I got to San Diego what I was going to do with the bike and all of my gear. Maybe I'd come up with meeting a new friend at the end of the road, and they'd help me store the bike? Unfortunately, I didn't know a single soul there. Then, just the thought of meeting someone, even in Oklahoma, was pretty intimidating, as I was very shy growing up. Similar to my pet turtles when I caught them to say, "Hi, I want be your friend," then they clammed up and closed themselves off from the rest of the world. Like for people, I couldn't think of how to open them up and convince them it was more fun to risk losing one's shyness and not worry about being vulnerable to possible embarrassment.

CHAPTER 12

HELPING HAND IN TEMECULA

L ooking back on trying to survive, enduring the winter elements, my lack of food, lack of money and not having shelter when needed were all answered by the new people I met on
the spot, and out of the goodness of their hearts they gave to me,
knowing they wouldn't get anything in return, except to feel all
the happiness inside making their generosity worth it all, helping me make it possible to reach San Diego, California. They ex-
emplified the motto, "It's more blessed to give than to receive."

Through this long journey, I realized I had broken my shell
of shyness. I realized that I would not have gotten anywhere if I
hadn't overcome my shyness by reaching out in boldness.

After riding with a lot of fast-paced drivers for the day, I
came into Temecula, California, at sunset, trying to find a place
to knock off for the night. There was a town square building
that resembled the Alamo, which had a waiting bench for visitors that I thought I could make into a sleeping bench. It was
still pretty cold, so as darkness enveloped the city, no one was

hanging around disturbing my peace and quiet. The businesses along the street become randomly dotted with lights inside their storefront windows. Like most towns, all of the marketplace workers and customers commute to the residential areas after 6 pm. Since this was my last night on the road before rolling into the gates at MCRD, I hoped for a deep sleep to rejuvenate my system for the Marine Corps qualifying physical.

The morning came with the early bird merchants rolling into their stores to open for business and waking me up. There was something about the presence of people in a new place that made you feel uncomfortable just lying on a bench, so I sat up quickly, like someone had pressed a button to an electric shocker to get me jump-started for the day.

A nicely dressed man came up to me and asked if I would like to have some toast and an orange juice. Yeah! Then he said, "Just wait here for a minute and I'll be right back."

"OK," I replied. He must have thought I looked homeless and didn't have anything in life.

As he walked away, I could see he was going to a little coffee shop just a few doors down. He brought back a whole bag of stuff. He said, "I hope you like this."

So I looked inside and wow, there was just not toast and orange juice, but a banana and a donut. Then I said, "Yes sir, I will, I'm pretty hungry, thank you so much."

He exclaimed, "You're very welcome!" He turned and went back into the coffee shop. I was convinced he was very a caring man. I wolfed down the entire bag and drank down the orange juice.

My "energy cells" had been charged up for what I hoped to do today—that is, for this whole trip to culminate in reaching my ultimate goal of being the only man in the United States history to ride a 10-speed 1500 miles into a Marine Corps base in San Diego.

The Palomar Mountains were off in the distance in the eastern morning sky, where they had the famous Palomar Observatory, which had one of the world's largest 200-inch mirrored telescopes with the ability to open the door to the many unknown mysteries in outer space. For instance, will we see other planets with life on it like our planet Earth? Will we find aliens or any kind of activity in outer space, such as alien spaceships or UFOs? It would be amazing if astronomers were looking at one of the planets and saw something move, discovering life of an unknown kind stirring about. There has been the fascination with observations of the universe's colorful planets, stars, moons and constellations with all of mankind throughout history.

I made progress down Highway 15 and passed the turn off to Oceanside, which signaled the closest I had ever been in my life to the Pacific Ocean. It was tempting to take the 12-mile detour west from my route to see the sandy beaches, sea shells and rolling waves of the ocean for the first time, but I was more tenacious than a bull dog to complete these last 35 miles and not let anything get in my way.

I was likened unto a long distance cyclist in the Tour de France race, after completing the majority of the 2,200-mile course, when he's coming to the last section, having a myriad of thoughts motivating the mind, sending endorphins into a frenzy of excitement with feelings like I was going to finish in first place, I'm setting a new world record, the television cameras are rolling and I've got to look my fastest. That's why the last moments of the race are more important than the start. Therefore, I was motivated to crank the pedals harder with all the strength that I had left.

The clear blue sunny sky on this Sunday, December 31, 1972, was like warm open arms of a welcoming feeling that made me smile for both reasons of the momentous journey of a lifetime coming to an end and the close of another year's world history.

Continuing down "the home stretch" into the city limits of San Diego, I was jockeying over from Highway 15 to Highway 5, which should bring me into the base. As I traveled faster into the area, I found Old Town San Diego, a State Historical Park, but had no time to tour and explore. I was running late into the day, trying to take the right turns and get into the gates. After a couple of more miles, I saw the first view of the huge Marine Corps Recruit Depot, which was like a gigantic industrial plant. There were hardly any cars around and nobody walking around, but woohoo, I saw the stone arches over the entrance with the Marine Corps emblem. I rode through the gates and to the doors, but questions started popping up in my mind. Where was everybody? Where were the crowds and the cheers of victory? Would they not have a Marine Corps reception party?

I parked my bike, leaning it on an entrance pillar, walked up to the huge doors, and I found them locked! What day did they think this was, Christmas? Not a soul around. Just then, it dawned on me—THIS WAS NEW YEARS EVE!!! Everyone had taken off duty for the holiday. On an extraordinary trip like this, you usually never took time off for a Holiday. However, didn't they have my name to be here for my arrival? I was pretty ticked off and disappointed with the MCRD.

Here, I had survived and completed my 1500-mile journey, I just crossed the finish line, I accomplished a historical event and no one was here to even open the door. Just crap-o!" No recognition, no celebration, and no place to go. I couldn't exactly turn around and go back. I started thinking, what do I need to do next?

I didn't want my trip to be daunted by the Marines finding me plopped out on the front door steps like a cold sack of potatoes. So I turned around and headed out back past the Old Town San Diego State Park, to go to a local civilian neighborhood. I came up with a plan to find a new friend and ask them if they would be willing to store my bike and gear because I was going into the Marine Corps. Well, as it turned out, I was riding down a quiet street that had style of houses built with higher foundations, meaning they could have basements possibly. So I saw an older man sitting out on his porch, tossing a ball for his dog to play fetch. As usual, what do dogs like to do best? They either bark at or chase bikers. I was no exception. As the German shepard lunged out at me, I said, "Hold it there boy, I just want to be friends, I'm not going to hurt you."

Then the man commanded his dog, by saying, "Get back here, Sergeant! Leave him alone!" And you know that worked, Sergeant obeyed.

That gave me an open door to start talking to this new friend, by saying, "How are you doing, sir? What a coincidence! I was just looking for a 'Sergeant,' but more of the two-legged kind, such as a Marine Corps type. I actually rode my 10-speed 1500 miles to go into the Marine Corps Recruit Depot and just tried to enter in the gates but the doors were locked."

He responded, saying, "Yep! Since tonight is New Years Eve! They're probably out partying and living it up somewhere in town."

I said, "Well, I would not have known ahead of time, but I figure I'll have to find a way to store my bike and have a place to stay for one night. Do you happen to have a little area to put my bike?"

He replied, "My house and garage are packed out with my family, but let's ask my neighbor, Miss Christy. She's got a bigger house and even rents rooms to people. I'll put Sergeant in the house, and I'll take you over to her house."

His dog went inside without resisting, and his kids were yelling in the background. So he started walking over about two houses down from his, as I slowly walked my bike behind him. He went up and rang the bell, and this middle-aged lady came to the door and said, "Hello, Scott, What are you up to?"

He said, "Hi, Christy. I have someone here that you might be able to help out. He needs a place to store his bike while he's going into the Marine Corps and maybe you can put him up for one night. What do you think?"

"I've got a little room in the basement, if he can get down there. Do you want to go down and look?"

I thought, "Boy! How could I say no?" So I said, "Sure!" So I followed her to a door in the hallway to descend into a dimly lit, tightly packed area of pillars supporting the house. I assessed the right-side corner just had enough room to squeeze my bike in, among a lot of dusty old wooden crates that maybe had her own personal items and old shop equipment like a drill press, table saw, work bench, etc. So I climbed up the narrow, steep-pitched stairs to tell her that this would work if it was okay with her. She said for me to help myself and bring it on in.

Then I shared with her, "I don't mean to take advantage of you, but I'm going into the Marines for a couple of years and when I've completed my service, I'll come back and pay you for storage."

But Christy said, "I'm not worried about that, I'm just glad to be able to help you out. While you're putting your things in storage, I can fix you some beef stew, if you're hungry."

I said, "You just read my mind. You wouldn't believe it, I'm so hungry, I could eat a horse."

"I'm considering you my guest," she said. "I'll let you get cleaned up in the restroom, which is the next door down the hallway, and if you want, bring me your clothes and I'll wash them. Here's a bathrobe."

My goodness! How fortunate I'd become. I felt like she was giving me the full service treatment. As soon as I pulled off my clothes, I slipped on her bathrobe decided take advantage of her offer and gave her all my clothes. I got the hot water going in the shower to spray me down after going for so many days on the road. It was like a tingling massage, making me feel so good that it caused a tantalizing of my senses. The shower was both rewarding and relaxing.

Not having any clothes to wear, I thought I'd be brave in coming into the kitchen with nothing but her bathrobe on to eat dinner with Christy. I found her in the kitchen, where she exclaimed, "Well, aren't you more comfortable and feeling better?" This lady had everything I needed, as if I had planned ahead and paid her in advance.

After checking the progress of the washing machine, she instructed me to take a seat at the dining room table, asking me if I wanted some wine, Coke, or something else to drink. I told her, "I'm quite impressed, I barely know you, and you're treating me like a prince on his birthday. What will I need to pay you?"

Christy smiled real big and replied, "Hey! This is a special occasion. This is New Year's Eve! Don't you want to celebrate?"

"Wow! I guess so," I said. But in my mind, I never even planned to have any kind of a celebration, because my entire focus and energy was solely to enter the gates at MCRD. How in the world was this spontaneous opportunity even happening with Christy, whom I just met? Then I expressed to her, "I've never drunk wine before, but since you offered, I guess I will have a glass with you." So she brought out a bottle of Franzia Moscato which she poured in two glasses. "You know, Christy, we can celebrate two occasions: New Years Eve and the fact that I've completed my 1500-mile bike trip by January 1ˢᵗ to go into the Marines tomorrow."

After she had a couple sips of the Moscato, she was already bubbling over to say, "I'm having more fun doing this with you, rather than going out on the town just for myself, so let's make a toast together, to you, Daniel, for completing your trip and to a happy New Year." Then we tapped our wine glasses together twice and took long sips as we smiled deeply into each other's eyes.

We indulged ourselves in the beef stew, beans, mashed potatoes, and bread she cooked up for what had become a very surprising celebratory evening. During the course of our dinner, Christy shared how she became an independent entrepreneur selling beauty supplies, which supported her very well, but that her boyfriend tried to use the profits for his own business of trying to be a travel agent for vacation planning and even went on cruises, claiming that it required him to experience the trips personally so that he could sell better. But after about the sixth cruise he went on, to the tune of almost $10,000.00, Christy was saying, "That's way too much! I'm not going to let him to continue zapping my business earnings for him to have so much fun and then not have his vacation planning business hardly increasing profits for the two of us. So I broke up with him, and I'm happier now. Especially happier having you come to my house tonight."

Then I said, "Aw! Thank you for everything you're doing for me. This is more than I could ever dream would happen. You are quite the hostess with the mostess. Then I told her about my life in Tulsa, my love for motorcycles, water skiing, camping, building model cars, the pets that I've had, and training in building engineering.

We stayed up half the night, talking about everything in the world. I could see that it was getting really late, so I offered to clear off the dishes and wash them up. However, Christy said, "No! You're my guest tonight, and I'm treating you to a good time. You'll need to pull your clothes out the dryer though and put them away." She had made me feel so comfortable and relaxed, that it did give me a feeling like I was at home.

I told her, "I'd like to stay up longer and chat more, but I'd better see where you want me to sleep, if that's still okay?"

She said, "Of course it's okay, let me show you the way. First bedroom to the left is a small student décor, with a study desk. Second one is bigger with a more rustic décor, and the third is my bedroom. You can pick where you want to sleep, and I'll be coming back in after I finish up the dishes."

I said, "Alright, I'll get ready for bed."

Unzipping my backpack, I pulled out my toothpaste and brush to service my choppers. I slipped on some shorts to sleep in and snuck into bed before she came down the hall. I hoped I got the right bedroom she wanted me to be in. It was all in the dark and it was kinda scary being inside someone else's bedroom.

It got very quiet for a while, and then I heard footsteps coming down the hallway. Then BANG! BANG! She turned on the lights causing me to instantly react. Jumping out of bed, I yelled, "What was that! I thought I was getting shot!"

Christy laughed and said, "It's a New Year's Eve tradition here. The neighbors fire off their guns and set off their fireworks at midnight. Did it scare you?"

"You have to know it did," I told her.

"Well, let's get you tucked back in, it shouldn't last much longer. I hope you will sleep well. Goodnight, Daniel," she replied.

I said, "Goodnight, Christy."

Even though there were late night celebrations with all of the wine, guns and fireworks going off, making it hard to sleep, I found myself still waking up with the rising sun beaming through the window. I needed to get dressed and get myself down to the Marine Corps Gates again. I washed my face, pulling my clean clothes and boots on. I stuffed a few things in my backpack and headed down the hall, sensing the smell of bacon and biscuits.

Christy caught sight of me and said, "Daniel! Come on to the table and have some breakfast that I'm just finishing up with."

"Oh, I didn't mean to be so much trouble for you, but I do appreciate it," I told her.

Then she had a smile from ear to ear as she said, "I'm enjoying doing this for you, like my gift of service to you, and I figured you needed a breakfast to start this New Year."

I was truly touched by everything she did. We had breakfast together and discussed my coming back for a visit. I would like to bring her back something in the future.

Christy said to me, "Daniel, I know you'll have to leave your bike and gear here in my basement, so why don't I give you a ride to the Marine Corps Gate?"

Then I replied, "You've done so much for me and I greatly appreciate everything, but it's just a short distance of probably less than two miles. I think I'll do the walk for a change in perspective, after riding a bike for 1500 miles, and then I'll be glad to have had the bike and not having to walk the whole trip, if you can imagine that? The walk will give me time to reflect on everything that have happened, from the start to the finish, the changes in my life that's already happened and anticipate the literal change from being a civilian now to the transformation into a Marine Corps soldier when I go through the gates never to return again to my former life."

Christy spoke up to say, "Oh, Daniel, I like you just the way you are now. I don't want you to change anymore, but I'm proud of you going into the Marines."

I picked up my backpack and gave her a hug, saying, "Thanks so much for everything and I'll see if I get a military leave to come and visit you."

"Okay, I would look forward to that. I've written down my phone number and put it into your side pocket so let me know. Goodbye," she said.

CHAPTER 13

MARINE CORPS, HERE I COME!

I stepped out into the optimism of this new day with heightened excitement, encouraged by the brightness of the morning sun that this morning walk will be my last for this season of my lifetime. I was hoping for the Marines to receive me and knew well that I would be cut off from the world for the purpose of being trained.

I opened the door, entering into the bright sunbeams of the morning that would set my mood aloft into feeling optimistic about walking the final mile and thinking I was really ready to make this happen. All of the many adventurous encounters of the trip could be an exciting way of life, but for me, they were not enough to fulfill the amount of life change that I was pursuing. The many new discoveries I witnessed always promoted more curiosity to go further than my imaginations. I was like a new eagle hatchling, ready to leap from the edge of the nest on a mountain cliff to fly into a new world beyond the home nest. Once in flight, there were not many limits, and you eventually wanted to fly farther and higher in the sky.

As I was walking along the road in this neighborhood, there were kids riding their new bikes, waving at me, very likely what they got for Christmas, which already made me miss having my own bike again, because the Junet 10-speed that got me here was in a strange way like a faithful buddy, and I was attached to it. But I had to put "Buddy" to rest and go on with what the future held-for me, putting my life in the hands of the Marine Corps.

There was a drastic change in climate from riding through five states having winter, then going south here into San Diego, which was now like spring. I had always worn my coat and boots for the whole trip, but now I needed to shed them before getting overheated.

Just about three quarters of a mile into my walk, a car pulled up beside me and the driver spoke. "I'm going your way. Do you want a ride?"

I told him, "No, thanks. I'm just enjoying a short walk before I go through the gates of the Marine Corps Recruit Depot."

He replied, "Okay, have a good day."

I didn't know the people here were so friendly. I was given the impression from being told to watch out for Californian people out here because they were pretty wild. Well, so far, I was giving them a high rating for being so hospitable and nice. Even though I looked like a lone traveler, I probably stood out. Some cultures across the states just let you pass through without showing any interest or asking if they can help. So I did like California people, and I felt like I could open up to them. With the good vibes and warmth, I had a spring in my step, a hop in my walk, and a smile on my face. The string of residential houses quickly turned to commercial buildings near the outskirts of MCRD.

My morning trip had finally brought me to the "golden gates" of the Marine base. Following the driveway a little farther inside the gates brought me to the huge double doors that I came to yesterday, and now I found them unlocked. I walked up to the reception desk and said, "My name is Daniel Gabriel,

I'm reporting for duty, sir. I just rode a 10-speed 1500 miles from Tulsa, Oklahoma, and arrived yesterday, but nobody was here."

The desk sergeant responded, "You rode all the way here on a bike?" Yes, sir! "That's quite a feat. We might have our Marine Corps Journalist interview you later. But for now, Daniel, since you walked through those gates, you now belong to the government, and we will train you into being a United States Marine. You will have the new name of Private—Private Gabriel, and you will not speak unless spoken to, is that understood, Private?"

I said, "Yes, Sir."

The sergeant went on to say, "Your every move will be ordered by your drill instructors, and you must follow everything they say and command you to do. They will be your superior officers whom you must respect. Is that clear, Private?"

I said, "Yes, sir!" I was ordered to sit down until further directions were given. I later discovered their way of receiving recruits was by an off-site receiving station, where men took buses, cars, trains, planes or motorcycles there and then got shuttle bused over from there. When they arrived, the new recruits stepped down out of the bus and were instantly ordered to stand on a hundred rolls of single-file yellow footprints. Then the desk sergeant ordered me to join in and to stand on a pair of yellow footprints of my own. This was the start of the Marine Corps Boot Camp.

Many intense training procedures beyond description would take place over the course of the next three months. I, along with most of the platoon of about 75 men, would follow orders obediently, but it only took a few men to mess up, and the drill instructors punished the entire platoon. Their core mission of the instructors was to continuously "fight out the undisciplined nature" and snuff out any self-desired thinking in us. Then, as our very own self-willed traits were beaten out of us, the drill instructors hammered in their own strategically overpowering control tactics to follow. There was absolutely zero tolerance for anyone's behavior that was not conforming to the drill instructors orders, or "DIs" as they are called, who were always yelling. The phenomena of complete mind control over your surrendered will gave all Marines and military superiors 100% rule over anything we may think or do. Putting it in other words, the Marine Corps Officers, had us all trained to be so dedicated and loyal to carry out their orders, that each one of us would become like an attack and kill weapon of war—meaning they say fire! Then we were the physical rifles that they just pulled our triggers, verbally, to take out the enemies. Orders said, "March up that hill and take it by force!" Then we did it instantly, without fail and no other thoughts or options could change that. But if we possibly had our old self-willed reasoning, then we might say to ourselves, I'm not going up that hill because I'll be shot at and killed. If a private recruit disobeyed orders, at anytime, they were called traitors and could be court marshaled.

Sometime about the sixth week of boot camp training, the three DIs went ballistic with some of the privates being disrespectful and had became extremely brutal by punishing all of us when we were lying in our barracks beds. They pulled us out of our beds, ordering us to crawl on the floor like worms, calling us maggots, scum, and you filthy bums are not worth anything! After they were kicking us, yelling at us, punishing us for hours, degrading us continually, I didn't remember ever being the same again after they broke down our individual self-willed characters. So the DIs had successfully destroyed our inner confidence in our independence and attitudes to the past ways of thinking. The DI's drove out all of our self-worth and any mindsets that a person could have had. The DIs became our mental controllers—we learned that they would inflict pain if we didn't obey orders. It could be more painful than we could handle and force us into the survival mode. It was easier to think, "I want to do what the DI's saying," rather than to suffer pain and punishment. Just do it!

I had found a new life and had a changed life that I loved, just from the month before entering the Marine Corps. Encountering what the new world was showing me, I could sense the forces of encountering nature profoundly pulling out the Daniel from inside. I dramatically lost my life, that of being the "Adventurous Daniel," to be forced to become "Private Gabriel" for the Marines. But I had a feeling of wanting to get out because I was thinking, "I really didn't mean to sign up for this." But I'm committed to become: "One of the Few, the Proud, the United States Marines."

It's a true statement that I had heard since I got my first 22 caliber rifle at twelve—the Marines will turn you from a boy into a man. I'm living proof that it happened to me in dramatic form. The Marines always had the highest standards and the toughest boot camps in the world.

Rifle Training. This is a picture of me (on the left) and my fellow recruits training with our rifles.

Of the many experiences being in boot camp, some of my more favorable ones were going to the rifle range with my M14 and qualifying to be an Expert Shooter. Then going to overnight attack training and firing tracer rounds, which are glow-in-the-dark bullets showing where you are shooting. They're like an awesome laser light show with red-orange streaks going everywhere.

On one day, we hiked back into a jungle area to climb up a lofty eight-story structure with lots of ropes from the top to practice parachuting from the top. This simulated jumping out of a cargo/ paratrooper plane. You had to put your trust in the straps and the practice parachutes as you fell downward. I thought it was as much fun as an amusement park ride. Seventy-five of us made the climb up and then made the eight-story drop without anyone falling to their death.

After completing boot camp, graduating with honors, I was directed to be trained as a Communication Centers Operator, who carries radio equipment in the battle field for officers. I

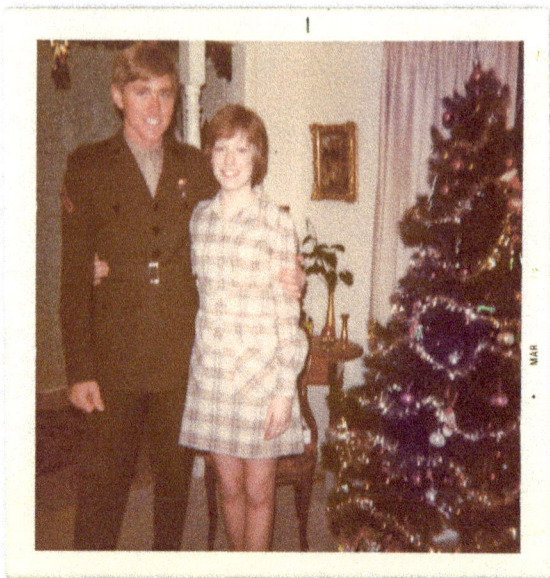

Sweet Renuion. After I completed bootcamp and before I reported to Camp Pendleton, I was able to go home to Tulsa to visit Mary Ann, my highschool sweetheart I left behind months earlier.

was transferred to Camp Pendleton for further training. The Marines had built this person into a "lean, mean fighting machine." I could aggressively "fight our country's battles in the air, on land and sea."

After serving several months, they selected me to do prisoner escort training, which is similar to MPs (Marine Police) carrying a 45-caliber pistol, and more self-defense training in Okinawa Karate, earning a Brown Belt. But what was completely unexpected was that I had to hold in arrest and escort a good friend of mine, Tom Case, who they said had taken off from his ordered posts and went into prostitution in Texas. He was captured and brought back to Camp Pendleton. The challenge was when he asked me to let him go secretly, doing him a favor as a friend. Sorry! Not a chance. I never saw it to be a good thing to let him talk me into something to his advantage and put me up to be court marshaled. So I continued to be faithful to serving in the Marines.

The commanding officers gave me orders to do deuce and a half truck driving and combat jeep driving training. Along with the operational instructions, they had shown on a screen a lot of fatal accidents with horrendous fiery crashes, which probably psyched us out on how dangerous these vehicles could be and that we must be orientated to emphasize mastering the driving skills needed because the lives of the officers and soldiers depended on us. The design of these vehicles required them to have a high center of gravity to clear going over very rough terrain and going through rivers, so they could turn over and flip easily going at a fast rate of speed or in turns.

After three weeks of intense training in the classroom, they turned us loose, putting us into ten combat jeeps to convoy out after the leading staff sergeant, heading into the backcountry wilderness and Camp Pendleton Mountains. We seemed to be driving into uncharted lands at a fast rate of speed that risked us going out of control. We slid through the switchback turns, flying over berms and rocks and whipping up the dust that was blinding us. Suddenly, all of the jeeps were crashing into the back of the jeep in front of them, not able to see ten feet in front of us, as we each slammed on our brakes. Then, when the dust finally settled around us, we saw the staff sergeant standing up at attention on top of the driver's seat, looking at us to count all ten jeeps and announce to us at the base of the mountain just beyond the end of the road were on, that this was King Kong

Mountain which had a narrow trail going up that had never been conquered. He was going to attempt to make it to the top today. This was Sarge's way of showing everyone who was going to be King of the Mountain and show what our combat jeeps are capable of doing or how close to deadly they could be. So he started up his jeep, revved it up, aligned to the center of the path, and stuffed it into first gear. When he dumped the clutch, the rear tires rooster-tailed dirt back into our faces, and off he went. He was charging the mountain like he was going to attack and slay a dragon with a giant sword with his jeep. The engine was screaming at the top of its power band as he shifts into third gear, getting the fastest momentum he could go, before hitting the base of the mountain. The jeep made contact with the very steep incline of the mountain, and the jeep's horizontal projection converted instantly to a vertical launch. Then we heard his engine sounding like a rocket engine thrusting with all the power it could possibly shell out, and about halfway up, he down shifted, jerking to the left, then the right. As he was spinning the rear tires, the front tires wheeled up. Now the engine was heavily grunting at the same time Sarge lost his momentum and his steering. The front of the jeep came up and over on its side, looking like it had flipped over on him. This was turning into the deadly demonstration version of what not to do.

But miraculously, it slid on its side and flipped back to the rubber side down and shiny side up. Well, then Sarge barely got his jeep back under control by locking up his brakes to keep from becoming another jeep-crashing casualty as he barreled back down the rough pathway. You could see the look of raging anger on his face coming from facing defeat from King Kong Mountain, which seemed like a sleeping giant to master the climb to victory, but turned out to be the unyielding ugly monster to him. We all clapped for him out of respect and for giving it the good old college try.

CHAPTER 14

COLLEGE, GIRLS, AND GUITAR

While I was stationed at Camp Pendleton, California, in the Marine Corps, I had a good friend of mine, Randy Actorhoff, with whom I did a lot of fun things on our liberty time together. We would go bowling, go to the beaches, and go to different places we had never been before. So, one day we decided to go on a trip to the San Diego Bay for canoeing for the first time. We bussed over from the base and found the place to rent canoes. We got two sets of paddles and life jackets with a bright yellow canoe. Then they gave us instructions to steer clear of other boats, staying within visible landmarks. We launched out into the deep waters, realizing canoes are very unstable, especially in a great big body of water with rolling waves from the Pacific Ocean. What we didn't expect, nor did we have any warning about was huge battleships coming into the bay, which is exactly what happened. A gigantic monster of a ship came at us. Had we ever felt so small? We tried to paddle away as fast as possible, looking like a small minnow trying to escape the jaws of a great whale shark. The combination of the ocean's waves rolling in and the battleship's waves being pulled in became insurmountable and overwhelmed us, rolling us over. We were instructed in case of capsizing to have one man on one side to pull the edge over and hold while the other man on the other side pulled himself inside.

I guess we had to practice keeping our weight in the middle all the time, or we could have become "shark meat," and I doubted that the sailors on the battleship would ever lower a life boat or throw out a rope. We were on our own.

My experiences of being a Marine were greatly rewarding during my two years of active enlistment. I was willing to do anything the military required of me: operate heavy artillery, crawl through the mud, or go wherever the mission was going to be—to serve and, if needed, ultimately die for my country.

I was awarded the Fireman's Badge, Sharp Shooters, and Expert Rifleman's medals. The officers over our battalion promoted me to the rank of Lance Corporal. Then after fulfilling my term of service, two years active and then six years reserve, the Marine Corps gave me an honorable discharge.

My love for motorcycles drove my desire to buy a 1972 blue and white Triumph Tiger 650, which I rode over to Christy's house. She was the middle-aged lady where I had left my 10-speed bike and gear. It had been over two years. I hoped she would remember me. I found the street she lived on, and the house was the same light blue siding. She had a lot of cars around, but I drove up beside them onto the sidewalk leading to her porch and parked on the sidewalk. She must have heard the thump of the exhaust pipes and saw me coming, because she threw the front door open and ran out yelling, "Daniel! I'm so glad to see you! You made it through the Marine Corps!" She wrapped her arms around me.

I responded, "Yeah, Christy, I always kept thinking about you, how we celebrated New Year's Eve and the completion of my 1500-mile bike trip. How could I ever forget that? You made that a very special time for me."

She said, "You know, it was a special time for me too."

Then I had to ask her, "Do you still have my 10-speed and stuff in the basement?"

She answered, "Well, come on in the house first and meet my brother and a friend."

I replied, "Okay, let me set my helmet down and comb my hair. Maybe I can get something to drink too?"

So we walked up a couple of steps and entered the living room, seeing two guys with long dark hair. Christy spoke up, "Daniel, I would like you to meet Wayne, my brother, and our friend Dave, who lives here now."

"I'm glad to meet you," I told them. Christy then stated, "Well, Daniel why don't you tell them about coming from Tulsa, Oklahoma, riding 1500 miles on a 10-speed, and that you joined the Marine Corps for the last two years while I get everyone something to drink."

Then I proceeded to say, "Well, guys, I had a vision and a life challenge to see if I could make it all the way on a 10-speed. If so, I felt that I would qualify myself to be accepted into the Marines." I shared a lot about the trip. After Christy had brought our drinks in, I finally got around to asking her about my 10-speed again.

She said, "Oh, Daniel! I have to tell you, I loaned it to a friend to ride on his bike trip out of town with friends, and he didn't bring it back yet. But your backpack and other gear is still in the basement."

I felt robbed at first, thinking awhile about it, then I decided to let it go by telling her, "Well, I don't have a way to take it on my motorcycle anyway, so I guess I'll just look at it like letting you have it as a gift to you, and you can keep it when he brings it back to you. You've done so much for me; we both can always remember each other through the bike. How's that?"

Christy said, "Aw! Daniel! That's so sweet of you!" Then she gave me a big warm hug.

Buddy, my 10-speed, also had a new life to make other people happy, but it was a little piece of the history of my life I shared with others and left behind. It was time to wrap up a good time of visiting with handshakes, and with a little good humor from Dave saying, "Guess you won't need your 10-speed anymore since you've got your faster version of a bike, so where are you headed?"

I replied, "I'm going to Sacramento College to study mechanical electrical technology and start a new life."

Dave said, "I wish you well and have a safe trip."

"Thanks!" I said. Then I put my jacket on and strapped on my helmet to get ready for the long trip. So I fired up the Triumph after a couple of kicks, mounted up, and carefully steered along the driveway to the street. I looked back to see them all wave goodbye as I waved back.

I was on the road again to another adventure in life by taking a 500-mile trip through new cities, new country, and a new experience, seeing new people, to live in the college town of Sacramento. It is also the capital of California. After the Marines had given me freedom again, I started it by my most favorite way—on a motorcycle. I've always wanted to explore the northern parts of California since hearing so much about it when I was growing up. This would be my longest trip on a motorcycle. I took Interstate 15, jogging over to Interstate 5 and up to make the fastest ride, figuring I would arrive before midnight.

The whole trip went pretty fast, however, for the last forty miles, the Triumph engine started making a scraping sound, which wasn't good. In mechanical terms, that probably meant a piston was scoring a cylinder. I tried to do more of a gentle and slower riding style. It paid off, as I exited Interstate 5 onto the historical

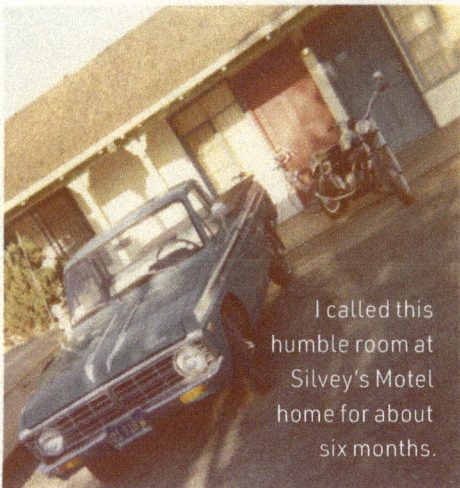

I called this humble room at Silvey's Motel home for about six months.

site of Old Sacramento, close to the Sacramento River. I pulled into Silvey's Motel, 1030 W. Capitol Ave. My motel consisted of an 8 ft. by 12 ft. room with a bed, table, and restroom. I ended up renting this room by the week while I was in the process of registering for college and finding a place close by, wherever that would be.

Upon reevaluating my trusty Triumph, the cylinders would have to be bored out one thousandth of an inch and first over pistons installed. Not having the money to pay a mechanic, I rolled my Triumph into my motel room, spread out some newspapers, and overhauled the engine right there with the help of a new friend, Woody, loaning me his tools, virtually turning my little room into a motorcycle shop.

I committed my next three years to studying and completing my Associates of Science degree in mechanical electrical technology. My veterans benefits covered my college tuition, but I needed to have funds to pay for books, rent, and other needs. So I worked three jobs: First one, as a motel clerk, the second, as a gas station attendant/mechanic, and the third, at Charlie's Hamburgers doing customer service. The motel clerk job was so interesting, as I encountered so many different people from all walks of life and from different places. At the same time, I could watch television and do my homework. I performed phone switchboard operations, which coincidently was the fundamentals of the Marine Corps communication work that I had been trained for. Assigning rooms, collecting payments, and helping people with their requests were some of the other job requirements. If I did the overnight shift, there was a single bed in the little room behind the counter. This was a rewarding position, giving me control over all the motel rooms and people coming in to stay.

After working for a year and saving up, I bought a Ford pickup truck and a Suzuki 400 motocross bike. I joined the Trail Bikers Sportsman Association. This was a serious elite riding group, taking us to extreme heights of the Mendocino Forest Mountains. We camped out for two to four days, took lengthy trail rides, and tackled some of the most sensational mountain climbs imaginable. We would see bears, coyotes, deer, and much more wildlife. When we were on top of the mountain ranges, we could see for miles, and it was so breathtaking! We even saw the snow-capped peak of Mount Shasta that was many miles away. There were so many awesome sights of nature all around us that it seemed like we were discovering a little piece of heaven.

While I was going to college, I met a very pretty girl, Barbara, who had such a lovable delightful personality. Music was one of her favorite interests with playing the guitar. For her, it came naturally to teach me how to play guitar. She opened up the whole world of music to me. She also connected me to the perspective of a deep appreciation for talented musicians that came to me while I was learning the fundamentals of playing guitar and singing some songs together. Enlightened by experiences of watching bands play, I became magnetized to see and listen to the guitar players do the finger placements on the arm of the guitar. It's a wonderful phenomenon in life of how we are touched by musicians producing music, and then it sings to our hearts perpetually.

Nothing beats having a glowing, crackling fireplace going,

Ten-speed touring continues. My college sweetheart, Barbara, and I did a bike tour through Yosemite Park, CA, near the famous El Capitan.

playing guitar with the warming accompaniment of an Irish setter and a cuddling girlfriend who loves you.

Barbara and I went to a big ski lodge in Squaw Valley with some friends to learn how to snow ski. Having some water skiing experience, I think that helped me maneuver the snow skis a lot better. The whole experience of going up into the snowy mountains, the beauty of everything decorated in white fluff, and even the big cabins covered in a foot of snow, gave me an element of being snowed-in, being forced into possible isolation. Along with everyone else's thinking, since we were all here with a group of friends, let's make the best of it together. Sleeping in bunk beds around the perimeter of a huge cabin was pretty unique. We had a great evening of a country dinner with wine and a live band playing for us to dance. The atmosphere was primed for socializing, with a huge group of young people indulging in eating, drinking, and being merry.

The morning came way too early, with the sacrifice of giving up sleep to do the late-night party hearty. We shuttled up to the ski lodge's equipment rental, where I learned for the first time about the necessary skiing equipment. The taller you are, generally, you will want longer skis, with the bindings adjusted for your weight to release your boot in the event of a fall. You select ski poles according to your height. Of course, you already know to bring ski gloves, goggles, insulated ski trousers, and a coat.

The excitement really builds when you snap your boots into the binding on your skis, and then you shove off with your ski poles to glide down a mild slope to the ski lift. You must anticipate the lift bench coming around, not stopping for you, but you have to push yourself ahead of the lift bench coming in back of you to sit down on it quickly. Then the reality of thrill or failure is going to take place at the top of the lift, getting off. You have to lean forward and push off from the lift bench quickly, or it may hold you hostage to carry you back down to the bottom, which would be pretty embarrassing. With the successful start, I felt pretty good. Now was the scary part: pushing myself to go faster and faster downhill. Being all tensed up, I probably looked as stiff as a concrete column ready to teeter at any moment and roll down hill. You can guess what happened next. I took off like a madman out of control and crashed! My skis went flying, and I found myself eating snow.

Then I had to crawl a ways down the slope to retrieve my

Skiing the slopes. I quickly realized what a thrill skiing was and made my way to the steeper slopes by day two of my first experience with the sport.

skis. Once I got down to the bottom, I decided to stop trying to look like I ski by myself and let a volunteer instructor show me how to stop and turn. The first most important maneuver for anyone learning to snow ski is called the snow plow which looks like a wedge or a V with the front tips of the skis coming together and the backs spread apart as you push on the inside edges to cause resistance, slowing yourself down. Practicing this technique, along with keeping your legs bent, helps you balance and steer. You have to get the feel of the metal edges of the skis before you can start learning to turn while keeping your skis parallel. After the first day of practicing the basics on the lower "bunny slopes," I made progress on the second day to the upper, more advanced, steeper slopes with moguls and sharper turns. From that point on, the world of snow skiing really opens up to a wonderful and thrilling experience to continue repeating because you find that you just can't get enough.

The time came that I became home sick for my family back in Tulsa, Oklahoma. I decided to quit my traveling refrigeration mechanics job, pack up my motorcycle and Brandy, my Irish setter, and move back home. I loaded up my truck and U-Haul trailer, cramming in as much of my stuff as I could, tighter than sardines in a can. I felt so loaded down that if I broke down or didn't make it to Tulsa, it would be because I was so overloaded. Confronted again with another do-or-die situation, I decided to try things out beyond what is known to be safe or previously tested. I was determined to go through with whatever may be encountered.

Driving conservatively, I sensed the engine laboring heavily with my gas pedal pressed almost all the way to the floorboard in fifth gear. Riding a heavily loaded 10-speed bike out to California over six years ago gave me the early western settlers, slogan of *California or bust.* Now I had the latest traveler's slogan reversed to *Oklahoma or bust.* Three days later, I rolled into my parents' driveway with the engine smelling like burnt oil and the cab like a sweaty doggie boarding kennel. Brandy and I were both elated and relieved to arrive in Tulsa. Hooray! We made it!

Here is my custom painted 650 Yamaha used for sport biking. Also, for many years, I had a 250YZ Yamaha to race motorcross.

CHAPTER 15

GREATEST NEW LIFE TO FIND

So much had happened since I left home in the six years of my life while in California experiencing major changes, never to be reversed or repeated again. This made me more of a different man than I was before: by daring to "jump off a cliff," which was pushing myself 1,500 miles on a 10-speed to San Diego, California; by joining the Marine Corps, willing to give my life for the service of my country; by taking a 500-mile motorcycle trip with basically nothing but a jacket and helmet to go to Sacramento City College. I found myself being a victim a number of times but fought back to be a survivor in this world. Inevitably, at various times through our lives, people will come at you, forcing you into being defensive, trusting, or they want to take from you, wherever you're living. I was thrown into the endeavor of discerning the ways that people can be good or bad and learning about the psychology of why people do the things they do.

I must say, for having so many experiences of all the world's display of overwhelming scenery that I saw, it may not even be possible to put them all into books and pictures. The many sights and wonders of nature that are untold and still to be discovered.

A lot of times I was awestruck to witness the unique environments people chose to live in and the lifestyles that formed their cultures.

I found it hard to put people's cultures I discovered into a justified description. Riding a bike allowed traveling at the right pace to see the most of the new world, and whenever I could stop, I could interact with people at the places wherever they lived. I would have never experienced the life-shaping that took place if I had taken a car, motorcycle, plane, or train from Tulsa, Oklahoma, to San Diego, California.

I did not know God personally or believe in Him before. But things happened for a reason. At age 26, I played church softball, encountering good sportsmanship and the invitation to come to a Sunday school class with the guys. Seeing how the guys played ball without the madness, hostility, or an out for blood attitude impressed me greatly by showing that they were changed and different than other guys. They became my friends. They were so welcoming, encouraging, and made me feel like an important player on the team.

However, my personal life was in a state of chaos, living a lifestyle of thinking it was okay to steal or secretly claim work tools as my own, lie about my actions, cuss like a sailor, go to bars to drink a beer, and get fighting mad at whoever. Then my first wife became very sick, developing some unhealthy conditions, and was going to have our baby. She became very angry and yelled at me, threatening to get a divorce. This became a huge burden falling on my shoulders, being hopeless to help my wife's health problems and thinking, *She's going to leave me and take everything, including our baby.* I knew that I had no control over her or the future of our baby coming into this world. I was suddenly aware of feeling terrible from all the wrongdoing in my life and even feeling guilty about all of the bad stuff I had done. Life's luck had run out, and I didn't think that I could live any longer with my own conscience condemning me. I had slipped into a bottomless chasm with no way out, like drowning in the ocean with no one to rescue me. I didn't know what to do or who to turn to. Things kept getting worse, and I wondered, how could it be possible to change things?

When I came to the Sunday school class one Sunday, my softball buddies pointed to something in the Bible people called the "Roman Road," which was mentioned in Romans 3:23: "For all have sinned, and come short of the glory of God;" also Romans 6:23: "For the wages of sin is death; but the gift of God is eternal life through Jesus Christ our Lord." Then Romans 10:9: "That if thou shalt confess with thy mouth the Lord Jesus, and shalt believe in thine heart that God hath raised him from the dead, though shalt be saved" (KJV).

This really stood out like a bright light coming on in my mind, and my heart realized three things: I was a sinner doing wrong, I needed forgiveness, and I needed Jesus to save me from death in hell. So I was convinced and believed that Jesus died for me and HE was raised from the dead to save me. God touched my heart right there in class, and I prayed with them, asking for forgiveness and confessing that I believed in faith for Jesus to be my Lord and Savior. LOVE, JOY, AND PEACE came within me, and the burdens of my sins felt like a ton of bricks falling off my shoulders. I had a life change from inside my heart that only God could do. I could smile big and be so happy.

Later on, God brought our family into better health, and we had a beautiful healthy baby girl named Christen Gabriel. We found happiness with a church fellowship and friends.

As it says in II Corinthians 5:17 (KJV), "Therefore, if any man be in Christ, he is a new creature: old things are passed away; behold, all things are become new."

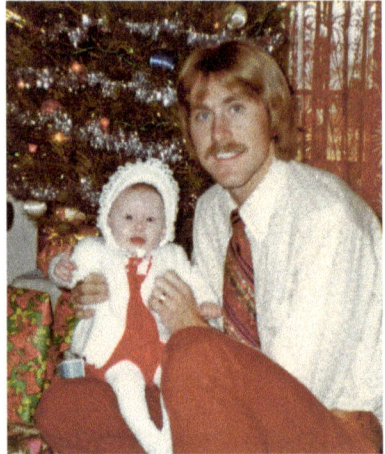

Me and my daughter, Christen, as a three-month-old baby.

I had become a new person. I wanted to stop lying, stop cussing, stop stealing, and stop doing wrong things. In fact, the Lord led me to take the tools back to the office where I had taken them from and ask forgiveness from those I had offended. My life truly changed for the good. Things got better with what God was showing me for my life. Looking back at the many near-death experiences or risks I had taken, like when I was on my 10-speed at night, riding without lights, then suddenly hitting an "ice rock," knocking me over and down in front of a semitruck, but supernaturally, I came back up—that was God's hand supernaturally picking me up instantly to save my life physically, to later save my life spiritually and discover that there is a real God in this world revealing Himself to me.

So I really did find a new life numerous times, with the discoveries of so many new experiences. But the most important purpose was that God wanted me to find new life in Him, as He gave me love, grace, and joy, that changed my whole world forever.

For the readers of this book, if you need to find that new life for yourself that God has for you too, then pray this prayer from your heart and soul in faith believing:

"Dear God, forgive me of my sins. I believe that Jesus died for me and was raised from the dead to save me. I want to ask Jesus to come into my heart and be my Lord and Savior. Thank you for saving me. In Jesus name I pray, Amen.

Our Family That Found New Life. My parents Leamon and Betty, my daughter Christen with my grandson Spencer, me, and my second wife, Margie.

The following scriptures are of particular importance to knowing salvation, and you may want to claim and retain them:

Ephesians 2:8-9: "For by grace are ye saved through faith; and that not of yourselves: it is the gift of God" (KJV).

John 5:24: "Verily, verily, I say unto you, He that heareth my word, and believeth on him that sent me, hath everlasting life, and shall not come into condemnation; but is passed from death unto life" (KJV).

John 3:16: "For God so loved the world that He gave His only begotten son, that whosoever believeth in him should not perish but have everlasting life" (KJV).

May the Lord GIFT YOU WITH NEW LIFE that will change your world and bless you throughout life with good things until eternity in heaven.

– The End –

But for some it's finding a new life that's actually a new beginning.